THE PURPOSE
OF LOVE

THE PURPOSE OF LOVE

A guidebook for defining and cultivating
your most significant relationship

DOROTHY RATUSNY

INSOMNIAC PRESS

Library and Archives Canada Cataloguing in Publication

Ratusny, Dorothy   The purpose of love : a guidebook for defining and cultivating your most significant relationship / Dorothy Ratusny.
Includes index. ISBN 978-1-897178-50-8
        1. Interpersonal relations.   2. Intimacy (Psychology) 3. Love--Psychological aspects. I. Title.
BF575.L8R28 2007   158.2   C2007-904517-0

The publisher gratefully acknowledges the support of the Department of Canadian Heritage through the Book Publishing Industry Development Program.

Printed and bound in Canada

Insomniac Press
192 Spadina Avenue, Suite 403
Toronto, Ontario, Canada, M5T 2C2
www.insomniacpress.com

For my father

Because I was fortunate enough to grow up experiencing the unconditional love that my father has for me, and because (with ease) he exemplified a loving and honorable male role model—someone who is intelligent, kind hearted, conscientious, generous, and strong—I have been able to go out in search of a relationship and a partner that would be all of the things that I knew were possible because of the man my father is. For this I am eternally grateful.

Acknowledgments

To this day, I continue to express my gratitude to the universe for allowing me to *find* Ryan in this lifetime. His endless love for me, his zany humor that repeatedly shows up at all of the right moments, allowing me (and so many others) to laugh hysterically at the silly in the ordinary, and his unwavering support and encouragement for me—far more at times than I would imagine possible—enables me to be all that I am.

Ryan lives by the law of "just." He is honorable in his quest for truth and accountability in all situations in his life and, at the same time, immensely compassionate and intellectual. As I have expressed to him many times, it is in his presence that I feel invincibly protected and "safe"—both physically and also in being who I am all of the time.

Ryan is—and always will be—my hero, my protector, my warrior, and my greatest love.

Heartfelt appreciation goes out to key individuals who together made it possible for this book to be out there in a "larger" way. Thank you to: Graham Fidler at PGC for being the positive catalyst in this incredible process by sending my first book along to "his friend" at Insomniac Press; Gillian Rodgerson for seeing the potential in my first project and for her great editing work, her honest thoughts, and comforting feedback; and Mike O'Connor for "green-lighting" this project, making it a reality.

To all of my clients, past and present, who have shared their life experiences, their innermost thoughts, and their life knowledge with me in a most incredible way. Some of your stories are compiled in the excerpts that follow. It is with gratitude that you have allowed me into your hearts and continue to have faith in my ability to help.

Contents

Prologue

Your capacity to love another human being—completely, with understanding and forgiveness—exemplifies who you are. Your love relationships are always reflective of the relationship you currently have with your self.

The greater your willingness to move beyond what you have always done and to challenge yourself to grow—to seek more from yourself and your life—the greater the likelihood that your relationships will be far more rewarding and honest (largely as a result of your desire to make them so).

Foreword

How many of us still long to be in a loving, healthy, intimate relationship—one that allows us to feel complete and whole… and loved?

On some level, do we quietly search for our "ideal" relationship, one based on media portrayals of complete strangers who cross paths at some auspicious, perfectly predestined moment and go on to experience an incredible rush of love, passion, and desire every moment that they spend together?

You betcha.

Blame it on Cinderella if you want, but at some point after the clock strikes midnight, the stylish, happily-ever-after fairy tale story gets horribly shattered. The simple notion that two people *can* build a life together and remain predominantly happy becomes replaced with one of uncertainty, mistrust, caution, and doubt.

We get married because we believe in the idea of true love and happiness, but the truth is that most of us haven't done all of the necessary work to ensure that the person we have chosen to be with is indeed the right person for us, based on who it is that we are.

Instead, we choose a partner based on what we have been taught to believe is important. We choose based on what we think will make us happy. We make choices out of fear, a false sense of security, or as a result of unrealistic expectations. We rarely choose based on what we know will support our happiness.

Our personal values are largely influenced by our cultural and societal beliefs, and present-day customs surrounding relationships and marriage are confusing at best. We continue to look for the person our culture tells us is the ideal partner with whom to have the "perfect" love relationship, even while all around us, we see evidence of how impractical and erroneous our expectations may be.

In addition to having an idealistic view of how our love relationship should be, we often overlook the connection between having this ideal and the actual work and effort that is required to create and sustain a healthy relationship.

Over our lifetime, our template for a healthy love relationship changes, ultimately because we are less willing to stay in relationships that are unfulfilling. We continue to search for the love relationship that will complete us, even while we still haven't figured out what that means. In the meantime, we don't actually know how to be happy with who we are.

℥

This book is for anyone currently in a love relationship, or in search of one. It is a guide to help you figure out what you need in order to be happy—with your self first, and then as part of a couple in a love relationship. Figuring out your true source of authentic happiness means that you can go about creating a love relationship that is built on what is most important to you.

As you begin reading this book and participating in the exercises, the honesty that I will encourage in you will uncover whether your current love relationship is what you need it to be. Your discoveries may mean making some difficult choices, but with the knowledge of what you want from your life (and from your love relationship) you will be better equipped to make informed and wise decisions that will allow you a life partnership that is based on love, joy, and mutual respect.

Furthermore, it is unlikely that you will come close to finding your ideal mate if you fail to identify exactly what that looks like. You may think that you know what you want in a life partner, but few of us have actually taken the time to sit down with a piece of paper and a pen to consciously list the qualities that are most important in an ideal mate.

Without knowing precisely what you are looking for, how can you expect to find it? Without knowing who you are, how do you begin to look for the right person to complete you?

Introduction

The most important element of a healthy love relationship is the ability of each person to operate out of a strong sense of self. Both need to have spent a considerable amount of time working on aspects of who they are as individuals, including such elements as: self-esteem; developing individual interests—both personally and professionally; and having sufficient life experiences as their "own person" prior to (and during) being together "in relationship." The couple's lives as single people inevitably allow them an opportunity to develop their sense of self as independent individuals with sufficient strengths—emotionally, psychologically, spiritually, and physically. From this, each is then able to share their self with the other.

In our current Western society, being "single" is often viewed with a certain level of negative stigma and single people are judged as being in some way undesirable.

And yet, to be "single" at different stages in your life is vital to building self-efficacy (by being self-sufficient and yet comfortable to be alone with your self). To be able to focus purely on developing your sense of self (aspects of your self-esteem as well as specific insights into what it is that allows you to feel happy) means that you enter into a relationship knowing precisely what you want.

Too often, I see clients who admit that they are experiencing situations and problems in their current relationship that are similar to those in past relationships. In order to figure out all the nuances of what we would like to see changed in our lives, and what we need to do to create that change, we need a heightened self-awareness and the feeling of self-efficacy that comes from the experiences of taking care of our self. This is most clearly achieved by living and being an individual on our own.

Most of us still look to the proverbial "love relationship" as the ultimate source of our happiness. This sets us up for the unrealistic expectation that someone else is responsible for making us feel good, which is wrong on all counts. Rather, it is through the realization that we alone are responsible for our happiness and that we can provide that happiness for ourselves, that we are then free to be in relationship without needing someone else to make us happy.

When we finally figure them out, our self-defined needs tend to be very simple. They include being able to do the things we most enjoy, feeling fulfilled, having a sense of purpose, and experiencing mutual love and the many luxuries that go along with that.

Instead, if you are predominantly focused on the needs of your partner and your love relationship, your sense of inner happiness becomes tied up with being part of a couple as opposed to doing the things that make you happy as an individual. Add children, a super-demanding work life, and aging parents to the mix, and our own needs get further and further ignored.

Once you have mastered the art of fulfilling your needs, not at the expense of others but certainly as an alternative to living vicariously through others, then you have the tools for making your current relationships more fulfilling and complete. Cultivating personal happiness (which comes from the effort you place on knowing and valuing the person you are and nurturing self-love) allows you to create the single most important relationship you will ever have—with your self. Enigmatically, it is the positive relationship that you have with your self that enables you to thrive as a couple.

Chapter One

Relationship Hype:
What's It Really All About?

All of your relationships have a purpose. None of them exist by coincidence. By embracing self-knowledge and growth as you navigate through your relationships, you learn immensely.

I can clearly remember a particular conversation that occurred on one of my many visits home from graduate school. As I sat at the kitchen table working on a research paper, I confided in my mother that I had just broken things off with my boyfriend of two years. Her expression quickly changed to one of genuine disappointment. With serious concern in her voice she asked, "Aren't you worried that you're not going to find anyone?"

Truthfully I wasn't. Finding another boyfriend (while certainly not my immediate focus at that very moment), and eventually a life partner was not something I had ever worried about. In fact, when I look back to the decade of my teens and twenties, I often wonder if perhaps I spent too much time being in relationships.

The Storm Before the Calm

My final storm before the calm was the tumultuous and messy ending of that same two-year relationship. I had intuitively known for a long time that this man was not going to be in my future. Yet, in spite of knowing this, in spite of our obviously different belief systems, cultural backgrounds, and expectations for sharing a life together, I was somehow determined to keep trying. I know now that a big part of what I was doing in trying to make things work was not unlike what so many other couples throughout history have done—and will continue to do. I was modeling the behavior that I had learned: two people in a committed relationship ought to work at making it work despite any obvious problems and ongoing, un-resolved issues.

I will always remember the pivotal details of my ill-fated re-lationship ending abruptly on the front lawn of my then boyfriend's home. It was the overdue finale of a long history of emotionally draining arguments that dominated the last several months of our relationship. My most vivid memory of that night was the incred-ible feeling of weight being lifted off my shoulders as I sped away in my jeep, with the top down, music blaring, and feeling the warm breeze of the late summer's night brush across my face. Knowing that I had left for the last time, I was, at that moment, in awe of the overwhelming feeling of freedom. I also secretly vowed to myself that I would stay single for a very long time. Little did I know what was waiting for me just around the corner!

The Simplicity of Ancient Practice

In Ancient Egypt, marriage had no legal or religious con-straints. There were no civil ceremonies, but simply a private agreement to cohabit with the person that you loved. A "marriage" occurred when two people decided they wanted to spend the rest of their lives with one another and made the commitment to live to-gether.

Love poetry from that same period indicates that couples chose their mates based on their feelings as opposed to formal arrange-ments. The informal act of "marriage" served to reinforce society's relationship between two people.

By the medieval period, women and men simply joined hands

and spoke explicit words, which in essence formalized the sacrament of marriage. Up until the late 16th century, priests and witnesses were not necessary for a marriage to be legitimate.

Since those times, marriage has been legalized and sanctioned by certain rules and regulations. Canon law defines marriage as a "permanent partnership ordered for the procreation of children" and "some form of sexual cooperation."

Traditionally, in patriarchal societies, children and property descend in the husband's line. The preferred method of acquiring a wife was through payment of a "bride price" to the woman's father in exchange for the children she would bring to the union. In most societies, marriages have been viewed as alliances between families rather than individuals, and the union has usually been formalized symbolically. Among Romans, Greeks and early Jews, gold wedding rings—perhaps the most common symbol of marriage—signified the groom's pledge of betrothal and were given as payment to the father of the bride.

Although the formal dowry tradition has died out in Europe and North America, the practice of negotiating a "bride price" continues in some societies, particularly in rural communities. Of the several kinds of marriages practiced in West Africa, "bond" marriages sanction the wife to become the property of her husband and children, as his heirs. If the husband should die before the wife, one of his heirs would "inherit" her.

Historically, few cultures have allowed individuals to choose their own mates. The majority of marriages throughout the world have been arranged by the families of the couple. Arranged marriages (which are considered a successful, traditional aspect of family life in many cultures) still continue in many parts of the world. Typically, parents arrange marriages in order to achieve a socially appropriate match and/or economic advantage. Often the bride, and sometimes the groom, has had no part in the decision. In many cases, the couple's first meeting takes place at the wedding.

While the institution of marriage appears rather inflexible in the way it is governed by societal rules and customs, modern-day civilization retains certain idealistic beliefs about the importance of committed love relationships and about marriage specifically. And yet, increasing divorce rates throughout North America suggest that either the institution of marriage as we have created it needs re-evaluating, or our beliefs and views about the purpose of marriage, and of love itself, needs an objective second look.

The Purpose of Your Love Relationships

All of your love relationships serve an important purpose in your life. Each has the potential to act as a metaphorical stepping stone—by bringing you one step closer to your ideal relationship. Each love relationship teaches you valuable life lessons. To learn these lessons means that with each relationship, you evolve in who you become and in your choices for an ideal mate.

In an altruistic love relationship, you are challenged to see your vulnerabilities, flaws, and errors, and yet you feel supported to improve upon them. What gives a love relationship meaning and purpose is its innate ability to encourage and inspire both partners to grow—to become more than what they were as individuals. In fact, it is likely that you are encouraged to become a better human being through learning about yourself, and observing and appreciating certain qualities in your mate.

> The purpose of your love relationship is to help you become complete—whole. Feeling "completed" does not happen because you have someone to *make* you feel that way, rather it is through being in relation with this particular person that you are inspired to learn, develop, and evolve—thus becoming more. Since your partner has the single most important influence on your present-day life, it is important that you choose, with full consciousness, the best person possible.

A healthy love relationship facilitates consistent growth and evolution. Even as it is your responsibility to remain consciously aware and to actively direct your individual growth, it is your partner's capacity to support, love, and encourage you that profoundly affects your ability to do so. You evolve by practicing present-moment awareness and then applying the knowledge that you gain from doing so.

Love relationships also teach you about ending points and how to acknowledge when a relationship no longer provides the mutually respectful environment that contributes to the integral quality of your life. To move on from your love relationship teaches you much about self-sufficiency and self-respect.

Purposeful Elements

The following elements are made possible through being in love relationships. This section is an overview, and these elements are expanded upon in other sections throughout the book.

A healthy love relationship challenges you to evolve.

Being in relationship requires that you think beyond your individual needs, openly communicate thoughts and feelings that you might otherwise refrain from sharing, and love without conditions. Because you and your partner have chosen each other based on qualities that you respectfully admire and appreciate, it is expected that you will both learn and develop aspects of yourselves as a result of being together. In a healthy love relationship (even if it does not end up lasting forever), you grow and evolve largely as a consequence of your varied experiences.

A healthy love relationship allows you to work on changing aspects of yourself, even though it does not demand that you change who you are fundamentally. Your consciousness expands as you experience your self honestly and authentically in the presence of someone who loves you, and you are able to come to your own set of conclusions about what you need to change and what needs to be different in order for you to be happy. Your partner supports the changes that you desire and is patient with you, just as they may be working on changing aspects of their own self.

Each of your love relationships further defines you.

If you allow it, your relationships can be the means by which you confidently explore your life. Each teaches you much about who you are and who you want to be. Your love relationships will consistently challenge your commitment to pursue and achieve your goals and dreams. You will at times need to choose whether you allow the relationship (and the goals and ambitions of your partner) to define your existence, whether you can mutually thrive by supporting each others' needs as individuals, or whether you choose to end the relationship, knowing that to stay would change the course of your life in a way that is not right for you.

A healthy love relationship is mutually respectful and supportive, and allows both people the privilege of achieving their individual goals and aspirations. Ideally, you and your partner come home at the end of the day to the comfort and safety of your relationship to share your challenges and accomplishments and to feel supported and encouraged by one another.

It is when you give up on yourself, denying your desires and ambitions, that you lose your self in relationship. It is when your identity becomes merged with that of your partner, and you settle for a life different from what you had decided for yourself, that you are then *defined by* your relationship.

Being in a love relationship enables you to heal
the wounds of your past.

The emotional and psychological wounds that you carry from your family of origin continue to affect your present day interactions with others. It isn't until you can experience being deeply loved and cherished by someone entirely separate from your family of origin – someone separate from the source of those originating wounds – that you can begin to heal from them. To heal from your past requires that you feel a depth of love that is comforting and trustworthy so that you can feel safe to experience similar situations with your family of origin or others, and to work through these with the reassuring support and encouragement of your love relationship.

For example, Jack's parents separated when he was four. His mother and father both remarried, and his father moved out of the country and began a completely new life. Jack saw him only once every seven or eight years. Jack's stepfather had four children of his own to parent, and so Jack never quite felt as though he had his stepfather's attention for long. Instead of feeling loved and cared for by two fathers, Jack was left on his own as both men were physically and emotionally unavailable.

Jack grew up feeling "let down" and abandoned in many ways by both men. He "quietly" continued to carry these hurts around with him, even though he had protected himself from the threat of further abandonment by creating an invisible barrier and allowing only select people in. As a single man, Jack didn't really have the full experience of looking at this childhood wound because his friendships did not require that he fully open up and share of himself for the purpose of healing. His relationships with friends existed and thrived without operating at this deeper level.

It wasn't until Jack was in a love relationship that he was confronted with the underlying emotional wound of abandonment. Whenever Jack and his partner, Leanne, had a serious fight, her initial instinct was to walk away, leaving Jack alone and feeling emotionally abandoned. Fortunately, he was able to acknowledge and eventually overcome his deeply embedded fear as it surfaced at different times, threatening the permanence of his love relationship.

In a love relationship where you allow yourself to be completely vulnerable, you do so trusting your partner to love you fully and completely. Even as you navigate through the challenges and problems inherent in all relationships, it is here that you heal from the hurt and pain of your past through the experience of having someone remain committed and loyal to you and the relationship. To overcome any of your earlier wounds from childhood is to heal from them.

Your love relationships have the capacity to teach you invaluable lessons, which will be significant in the rest of your life.

Your love relationships are wonderful for teaching you more about your self than you could ever learn independent of them. They have the potential for revealing, with honesty, the way in which your actions and behaviors affect others. Your love relationships offer many invaluable lessons: they challenge you to create healthy boundaries, understand differences, and learn acceptance. They teach you about the importance of self, since you need to take care of your own needs in order to be able to freely give of your self to others.

Your love relationships are healthiest when you can navigate them using your conscious awareness. To be consciously aware is to be present in your life and an active player in your destiny. Consciousness implies self-awareness and discovery. To be self-aware is to experience a connection to your inner self. In self-awareness, you easily recognize life lessons and apply these in creating positive change. Without consciousness, you find yourself in a constant flurry of reacting to what others "say" and "do." Without consciousness, you distrust or ignore your intuitive inner voice—finding ways to remain busy and distracted instead. With conscious awareness, you are reminded of the importance of achieving a balance that includes enjoying the experience of being in a relationship and simultaneously exploring and honoring your individual self.

Your most profound love relationship teaches
you unconditional love.

In your most significant love relationship, you appreciate that both you and your partner are perfect. (To love someone unconditionally doesn't mean that you are compelled to overlook their intense flaws or to allow them to treat you poorly and with a lack of respect, however.) Loving another human being unconditionally means that they can be who they are without having to behave in a way that suits your purpose. You love them in spite of the fact that they may not always close the screen door behind them (even when reminded), or that they may repeatedly leave their tools lying around rather than put them away. Your greatest lesson, outside of becoming more evolved in who you are, is being able to love another person without conditions.

Cultivating unconditional love for your partner helps you to do the same with others. Through your unconditional love, you teach others that they can be who they are (even if you may not agree with or approve of their behavior at times). Loving without conditions allows you to accept others without imparting judgment or negative consequences because they are not exactly what you deem they should be.

Chapter Two

Your Earliest Relationships: Hidden Messages and Meanings

Your template for how to be in a love relationship comes largely from your family of origin. As healthy or dysfunctional as that model might be, your way of operating in a love relationship has been determined by it.

As much as your parents provided the initial template for what a love relationship "looks like," it's critically important to examine exactly what you have learned from them. Because your internal operating system (what you know and believe) is largely based on the earlier programming of your childhood and your experiences within that environment, so much of what you innately recreate as an adult is unconsciously driven.

One of your biggest challenges is to implement an ideal balance of all of the "right" things you have learned (from your family of origin and your cumulative life experiences), and what you desire and believe to be the right way of being in relationship.

Identifying the largely unspoken and yet well-ingrained views and beliefs that you uphold is paramount if you want to understand (and even predict) your behavior in any love relationship. You can choose to emulate learned ways of being that are mutually respectful, loving, and that foster open and honest communication. You must also choose to behave differently in situations where your template—what you have always known—is less than perfect.

To be self-aware of all of the expectations and "rules" that you operate with is to reap the rewards of nurturing a love relationship that is more evolved, and more conscious, than what you have previously known.

Identify what traits and characteristics you innately search for in a partner and in a love relationship. Notice what thoughts and beliefs surround your need to be in relationship and what patterns continue to show up creating havoc in your life. To be aware of these is to consciously choose whether you continue to repeat old patterns and behaviors or whether you seek out and adopt new ways of thinking and being.

The Formative Years: Your Initial Relationships

Your relationship with your parents (and other important caregivers from your childhood) has the most profound effect in shaping how you initially see the world and who you eventually become. It is within this earliest relationship that you develop your initial impressions of your self, including how you experience your self in relation to others.

As children, we constantly absorb information about how to be in relationship from observing our parents and extended family. Because of our acute awareness, we pick up on such subtleties as body language, non-verbal communication, and underlying impressions. We also inherently know if our parents' unspoken messages are incongruent with their spoken words. Your parents and primary caregivers are indeed the single most influential source of what becomes your dominant model of communicating in relationships.

In initial meetings with new clients and as an important component of gathering relevant information about their personal background, I ask them to describe their parents' relationship, including how their parents expressed affection and love. As I also ask clients to relay details about their parents' personalities, they often acknowledge their awareness of specific character traits and ways of being that they directly observe in themselves that have been influenced in some way by one or both parents.

For example, if you were raised in a home where both parents typically modeled healthy behaviors and ways of relating (including respectfully disagreeing and arguing with appropriate resolution), then you have had an opportunity to learn tools for skillfully communicating in relationships. Consequently, if you were surrounded with unhealthy examples of how to communicate, an absence of displayed respect for differing views and opinions, and inappropriate ways of resolving conflict, you are likely to adopt these as "normal" ways of relating to others. And of course, communication becomes even more difficult and problematic if both people within a love relationship are operating with differing or even opposing belief systems.

Your personal template for how to be in a love relationship comes largely from your family of origin. Regardless of how successful you might perceive that model to be, it's important to examine and question the many social mores and cultural beliefs that you have accepted as correct up until this moment. By choosing how you want to be in your love relationship, you inevitably practice greater consciousness and take responsibility for your behaviors.

Your earliest formative relationships also played a role in shaping your current vulnerabilities and insecurities. Examining some of your earlier life experiences, you begin to identify the origins of your most disabling wounds. You can move past feeling emotionally vulnerable and powerless when you begin to challenge the perceptions and beliefs that you have held up until now. If you continue to live governed by your past negative or traumatic experiences (and remember that your personal assessment of them may or may not be wholly accurate), your earlier experiences become the emotional, physical, and psychological barriers that stifle growth.

As a result, you react in your love relationship as if all of your wounds are current rather than part of your past. By recreating your past, you can never move forward. You never experience what a healthy love relationship has the possibility of being.

My client Kody described his mother as extremely controlling and emotionally unavailable. Kody recognizes that he was often angry with his mother for her inability to care for him, as well as her lack of emotional availability. Kody's mother relied on him, the eldest of three boys, to be a caregiver for his brothers. Some of his regular responsibilities included making meals for his siblings and walking them to and from school. Kody was visibly sad as he recalled that his mother never displayed physical affection toward him. Kody never heard his mother say that she loved him.

Although Kody maintained a loving relationship with his father, he saw him as weak and vulnerable. Kody's mother quite openly had affairs and would often flaunt them in front of his father. Kody decided from an early age that his mother had more power in the relationship, even though the way in which she acquired power was undesirable. Kody's father was emotionally powerless since he could not bear to leave his wife and family, and yet he lived with the immense pain of knowing his wife did not love him in the way that he loved her.

As an adult, Kody quite unconsciously repeated the same pattern in his own love relationships. He was unfaithful in his marriage and in subsequent love relationships. It wasn't until Kody examined the unspoken messages inherent in his family of origin that he realized he was protecting himself from the possibility of being hurt. Kody behaved in the only way that he knew would allow him to maintain power in his love relationships. While Kody loved his father, he could not respect the fact that his father never confronted his mother over her incessant infidelity. Unconsciously, Kody aligned himself with his more powerful parent. Because he never wanted to experience the intense emotional pain that he had seen his father suffer, Kody would simply not allow himself to commit to a single woman. In his efforts to avoid being emotionally hurt, Kody's behavior was making it impossible for him to experience the kind of love that he so deeply wanted to feel.

Recognizing your earlier life experiences as a particular framework for how you see the world is important. As an adult, you have the ability to deconstruct your earlier learned beliefs in order to determine if they fit with what you now know. Realize that who you are is largely tied up in a learned way of being that is no longer applicable for who it is you want to be. Begin to feel empowered to make changes. Your search for inner happiness will motivate you to create a different destiny for yourself.

Her experiences growing up in her family of origin taught Chloe that she needed to be perfect. Chloe was reared in a home where her father and mother would frequently have heated fights, after which her father would simply storm out leaving her mother and siblings to fend for themselves for extended periods (days, sometimes weeks at a time). As the youngest child with four older brothers, Chloe recalls feeling responsible for her father leaving. In order to combat this, she did everything possible to be a perfect daughter when he was around. When her father was absent, Chloe's mother went into terrible bouts of depression, spending little or no time with the children. She would often lock herself in her bedroom for several hours, leaving Chloe to take care of her brothers and much of the housework and cooking.

Fast forward to present day: Chloe has recently made the decision to leave her own marriage. Her nine-year relationship with Christian has been a roller-coaster ride of emotional and psychological anguish. Recently it became physical when Christian shoved Chloe into a nearby wall during one of their arguments.

Christian admits that he is a very angry person, but blames Chloe for making him angry. Christian frequently takes his anger at the world out on Chloe and their children. He admits cheating with numerous women whom he met when on tour with his band but claims he did this when they were having trouble in their relationship and were essentially "on a break."

It is no coincidence that you end up in love relationships that parallel the relationships in your family of origin. Once you begin to see the familiar patterns between what exists in your current love relationship and what you experienced and learned growing up, however, you can then begin to identify and examine the ways of being you have learned and become accustomed to. Being consciously aware of how your all-too-familiar, albeit painful, surroundings parallel earlier life situations is necessary before you can begin to create change.

For Chloe, the dynamics of her parents' relationship coupled with the unspoken messages that she received growing up, served to create the working belief system that she held for how relationships should be. This was her relationship template.

On an unconscious level, choosing Christian as a partner meant that Chloe would recreate a familiar role to what she had always known. Striving to make Christian happy (or at the very least, to prevent him from becoming angry) meant that Chloe could forgive Christian's repeated bad behavior. When Christian became angry and lashed out at her and the children, Chloe blamed herself: she allowed his continual cheating, lying, and his lack of devotion to the relationship because it was what she believed was acceptable.

Chloe also believed she was happiest when Christian was happy. In focusing much of her time and energy on supporting Christian and building his self-esteem (often at the expense of her personal feelings of self-worth), Chloe had far less of an opportunity to do things that made her happy.

Because you unconsciously choose partners with similar attributes (both positive and negative) to your parents, you inevitably find yourself in situations where you face similar experiences to those in your family of origin. If you can recognize when your thoughts and emotions trigger well-rehearsed knee-jerk reactions in your current relationship, you can begin to understand and learn from these parallel experiences. With greater understanding and insight, you can then begin to figure out what you need to do differently in order to heal earlier wounds.

For Chloe, therapy was a place to begin to untangle herself from Christian. Because so much of her sense of self was tied up emotionally supporting Christian, and in feeling responsible (and affected by) his uncontrollable anger, Chloe had little invested in her own sense of self.

As we worked together, Chloe began to acknowledge the many other gifts she had to offer, one of which was her contagious, enthusiastic, attitude to life, which others gravitated towards. The large network of people who knew and loved Chloe also provided her with a great source of helpful contacts when she began to pursue her longstanding dream of being a professional photographer.

Fortunately, Chloe ultimately learned how to know and honor her self so that she could figure out and do what would make herself happy. By paying closer attention to her own needs, Chloe acknowledged the emotional strength that she had always had, and began to invest that energy and strength in developing her own sense of self, separate from Christian. Over the next three years, Chloe's career flourished and her daughters watched their mother outwardly become the strong, independent woman that they knew she was.

Today Chloe arranges visits with her daughters to spend time with Christian, although that remains her only form of contact with him. Chloe continues to work on believing and owning her many incredible abilities, and trusting herself to know what is right for her. From being in relationship with Christian, Chloe learned that she can be perfect (by her own definition) for herself without needing to be that for anyone else. Healing for Chloe has meant that she now addresses her own needs, and pursue experiences and opportunities that provide her with personal happiness rather than working so hard to please others at the expense of herself.

Learning valuable life lessons as you heal from your initial relationships in your family of origin doesn't necessarily require you to remain in your current situation. Sometimes the life lesson requires your ability to move out of your current relationship as you work on what you need to do to heal.

Re-examining What I Have Learned from My Earliest Relationships

Answer the following questions in as much detail as possible. You may want to come back to these questions again, building on your initial answers as you recall additional information from your earlier life experiences.

1. What have my earliest relationships taught me about self-love and my experience of who I am in the world?

_____

_____

2. What are my inherent beliefs about love relationships? From where did I learn these?

_____

_____

3. Which of the above "inherited" beliefs do I need to re-examine or challenge? (Which of these well-ingrained beliefs no longer serve who I want to be or what I want from my love relationship?)

_____

_____

4. What are some of my old patterns that I no longer want to hold onto? For each of these old patterns, how do I want to behave instead?

_____

_____

5. What would be the outcome if I behaved differently in my life, and in my love relationship?

_____

_____

Growing up: Establishing Your Experience of Self

Core beliefs are the absolute ways of thinking about yourself, others, and the world. Between the ages of three and five, the majority of your core beliefs have been established. Each of us is imprinted with core beliefs that are positive as well as problematic and negative. The positive ones ("I'm a good person," "I'm a generous person," "I'm a caring person") nurture healthy self-esteem and self-worth. They reinforce your belief in your favorable qualities and your inherent good.

Problematic core beliefs are typically inaccurate and irrational and keep you "stuck" in defeating patterns. Believing that you are "not good enough," "unlovable," "stupid," or "unworthy" creates self-imposed limits and reinforces a lack of self-confidence and low self-worth. Because core beliefs are the underlying mechanism influencing your thoughts, what you *believe* to be true about yourself is more important than what actually is true.

If you could rid yourself of your deeply rooted problematic core beliefs, it would free you to embrace different challenges, enable you to feel better about the person you are, and it would mean that you would look for an ideal partner rather than settle on someone who is "not so bad" or "okay."

Your core beliefs constantly influence your thought process. You perceive situations and events based on the core beliefs that you hold. For example, if you believe that you "aren't good enough" or "are flawed" in some way, your expectations in choosing a mate will be very different than if you believe you "are deserving" and "more than good enough."

For example, if the hidden (or not–so–hidden) message was that you "needed to be academically superior to others," and if you perceived that "you didn't measure up" to the standard your parents decided was acceptable (particularly if you wanted to please your parents), then it's likely that you would begin to believe you "weren't good enough academically." This message doesn't need a lot of rehearsal to become instilled as a core belief. Consequently, if left unchallenged, this core belief will continue to affect your thoughts and perceptions—particularly as it relates to your intellectual ability—throughout your adult life.

The underlying meanings and messages that you internalize as a child are communicated without knowledge of their critical impact. You don't need a clear memory of the various incidents and situations that contributed to developing a negative or irrational core belief. You only need to identify the core belief as having permanence and meaning to your life.

The Origin of a Core Belief

You race home from school, excited to tell your parents about the 90% you received on your science test. In a matter of moments, however, all of your excitement is gone. You happily share your great news, only to hear your mother say: "What mark did Julianne get?"

Julianne (the class "brain") just happened to let you know that her score was 94%. When you innocently convey this bit of information, you hear the words: "Well, maybe you could try and do better than Julianne next time?"

Your inaccurate core belief of "not being good enough" has just been negatively reinforced. If your parents placed a high emphasis on academic success, while growing up you would have received this message repeatedly.

At this point, your grade of 90% has been devalued. You have forgotten about your own (high) achievement and are now thinking about what it will take to beat Julianne on the next science test.

Although only in grade three, you are already learning how to diminish your success by believing that whatever you are able to achieve is "not good enough." You unconsciously reinforce this core belief long before you reach adulthood (and without even realizing that you are doing so). Instead of acknowledging and appreciating your accomplishments, you instinctively compare yourself to others who are more successful than you in some ways and focus on how you don't measure up.

Here's where it gets really interesting. This same core belief affects you in all of your love relationships. You feel not good enough when you compare yourself to others on one or any of the following: intelligence, career success, financial standing, physical attractiveness, and sexual appeal. You continually disregard your abilities and achievements and eventually, if you don't seek help to mitigate this behavior, your self-effacing thoughts (and beliefs) begin to create your outward reality. You unconsciously believe that you are "flawed" and "not good enough" to have the kind of relationship that you want, and so you continue to date people who are not right for you. If you are already in a love relationship, your problematic core beliefs continue to affect how you feel about yourself and you end up unconsciously sabotaging your relationship.

Irrational core beliefs create insecurity, self-doubt, and unsubstantiated fears. As a result, you become reliant on the reassurance and positive reinforcement of your partner to feel better (even if it is only temporary). It becomes very challenging for a couple to develop their relationship to its highest potential when one partner doubts themselves so fully. If you are single, your choices in a mate reflect your irrational core beliefs. You settle for far less because you have convinced yourself that you aren't good enough to be with the kind of partner you really want.

In a related but separate example, perhaps you grew up experiencing a great deal of criticism and disparaging comments, again regarding your academic performance. You heard remarks like these:

"How come you didn't do better?" ... "You should have got 100%!" ... "What is wrong with you?" ... "What happened to your brain during the test?" or "Why can't you do as well in school as your sister?"

After a time, you begin to believe that you are less smart than others. The reoccurring disparaging remarks cause you to doubt your ability. Even though it is far from the truth, you have already begun to adopt the core belief that you are stupid. By the time you get to high school, you are convinced that there is no point in taking courses in the advanced stream because you don't believe that you are smart enough.

Operating with this core belief means that in your love relationships you settle for whoever pays you some attention. You poke fun at your own intellect (but feel hurt when others do the same), you continually doubt your intelligence and abilities in the relationship, and you assume that you are not as smart as your partner without ever exploring the validity of this belief. Your love relationships and the destiny of your life are deeply affected by what you believe to be true.

Regardless of the origin of any problematic core belief, it is your responsibility to change it. Remember that you alone decide what you believe to be true.

Consider what may be one of your limiting core beliefs. Ask yourself: "Is this core belief who I really am?" and "Is this core belief accurate based on who I want to become?"

Given a choice, most of us wouldn't want to go through life feeling limited in who and what we are. Challenging your limiting core beliefs simply means having a closer look at what you have always accepted without question up until this moment.

Your core beliefs are the driving force behind how you think. Your thoughts ultimately determine how you feel about yourself, and what you do or don't do. In a perfect world, your thoughts would never be "limiting" or "self-defeating." You would instead believe in your ability and in the fact that you can accomplish anything you put your mind to.

Identifying Your Limiting Thoughts

List all of your limiting or self-defeating thoughts.

_____

_____

_____

How do these thoughts make you feel?

_____

_____

_____

What core beliefs are at the root of these thoughts?

_____

_____

_____

Your Thoughts

What you think determines how you feel and what you do.

As one of the most widely researched and practiced models of psychotherapy in the world today, Cognitive Therapy is the preferred approach for many therapists. Cognitive principles are easily learned and used in resolving a wide range of problems and situations that clients bring to the therapy session. The primary focus of this model of therapy is in establishing greater awareness of your thoughts, or "self-talk" (the constant and ongoing conversations you carry on inside your head) and the impact of these thoughts on your feelings and behaviors.

When clients realize the significance of their inner thoughts in creating their feelings and behaviors, they become far more empowered to pay attention and to choose the way in which they think.

Knowing that your thoughts play a determining role in how you feel and consequently react is helpful as you navigate within your love relationship.

To illustrate the role of your thoughts on your feelings and behaviors, consider the following example:

The Situation:

Tina's husband, Pete, is talking about his best friend's wife who just gave birth to a healthy baby boy. Pete comments on how he can't wait to have a son of his own and asks, "When do you want to start having children?"

Tina's immediate **thoughts** (her perception and interpretation) about what Pete is saying:

• "He's pressuring me again."
• "Why is he bringing this up again now? We just spoke about it at length a few weeks ago, and I told him how I felt."
• "It's so easy for him to think about having kids—his life won't change at all!"
• "I don't even want to discuss this."

How does Tina **feel** in this moment?
• annoyed
• angry
• irritated
• resentful

Now, think of a situation that remains unresolved between you and your partner. Perhaps it's an ongoing difference of opinions regarding the level of cleanliness in the kitchen. Or, the issue may be more noteworthy, such as whether or not you will have children and when might be the right time to do so.

Regardless of why this problem remains unresolved, recall the typical (and likely reoccurring) discussion that takes place. Think about some of the key points that you and your partner have frequently debated. Now, let's take a closer look. Record your thoughts and feelings together with a brief synopsis of the issue at hand:

The Situation:

_____

_____

_____

_____

What are your immediate **thoughts** (your perception and interpretation) about what your partner is saying?

_____

_____

_____

_____

How do you **feel** in this moment?

_____

_____

_____

_____

Since your thoughts create your feelings, pay attention in moments when you feel a strong emotion. Your thoughts and perceptions in a given situation provide you with important information about why you feel the way you do. To track your thoughts requires that you be consciously aware. You need to be able to recognize moments when you feel a strong (uncomfortable) emotion and ask yourself, "What was I just thinking?"

Your Feelings

A fundamental principle of Cognitive Therapy is illustrated in the linear equation below.

Thoughts➡Feelings➡Behaviors

This is a particularly helpful concept when you consider that your behaviors (your actions and reactions) are determined by how you feel. Your feelings are created by the way in which you think about, or perceive a given situation. Being able to articulate your feelings takes practice. It requires you to be consciously aware and at times, to sit with whatever it is that you feel long enough for you to be able to put words to your experience.

Look back to the example that you recorded earlier. Notice how your thoughts and perceptions were instrumental in creating your feelings. During each waking moment, you experience a constant stream of ongoing thoughts. (Each of those thoughts is created in less than a millisecond.) Understandably, it becomes almost impossible to track every thought as you experience it. (This is why recording your thoughts on paper—at least initially—is so helpful.)

Feelings (and emotions) are incredibly powerful. For example, in moments when you experience a range of intense and overwhelming (difficult) emotions, it can feel like they overtake you, as if you have no control over them. What we don't realize is that our feelings (and the intensity to which we experience our feelings) are created by our present-moment thoughts. (Of course, it can be very difficult to think positively if we are faced with a grave or tragic situation.)

You can actually increase the intensity of a feeling as long as you continue to think in the same (or similar) way. Your feelings also have the propensity to affect future thoughts, much like a feedback loop. For example, when you feel happy (a positive feeling), you are more likely to interpret situations and experiences in your life as positive. Since your thoughts are positive, you continue to feel happy, which then influences future thoughts. Conversely, if you are experiencing a particular low mood, it is likely that you will interpret events and situations from this perspective, which further perpetuates your low mood.

Cognitive therapy reinforces the importance of being consciously aware of your thoughts and of challenging your thoughts to ensure that they are based on accurate information, rather than on assumptions or speculations. When you create your own story about any given situation, you experience feelings that are created by your perceptions—even though your story isn't rooted in factual evidence but rather, your particular point of view, your present mood state, and influenced by your previous life experiences. As you learn strategies for critically examining your thoughts as a way of understanding why you feel the way you do, you begin to see evidence of how your mood state is completely determined by how you think.

Your Behaviors

Your behaviors are your actions and reactions. They are what you do. If you feel angry and hurt in the midst of a major disagreement with your loved one, you might react by saying something that is hurtful, slamming the door as you retreat to your bedroom, yelling, or crying. All of these actions are considered your behaviors. How you behave in any given moment is based on how you feel. How you feel is the result of your thoughts.

You have the ability to change the way you feel and behave by changing your thoughts.

You change your thoughts by challenging them.

Challenging your thoughts requires you to be consciously aware. You must be able to step back in moments when you feel overwhelmed by unpleasant emotions, or when you react or behave in a way that is not how you want to be, and ask yourself, "What was I just thinking?" as a way of uncovering the origin of your feelings and behaviors.

Recording your thoughts is a helpful way to identify exactly what caused your feelings and behaviors. When clients do this exercise in a session, they are usually surprised to see how their thoughts (even if they are inaccurate or illogical) can have such a powerful effect on their behavior.

A helpful strategy for challenging your thoughts is *the sentence stem: "Where's the evidence?"*

Using the earlier example, Tina would apply "Where's the evidence?"' as follows:

- "Where's the evidence ...that Pete is pressuring me?"
- "Where's the evidence...that I told Pete (and that he understood completely) how I felt?"
- "Where's the evidence...that it's so easy for him to think about having kids?"
- "Where's the evidence.... that his life won't change (with kids) at all?"

Let's deconstruct the above questions created out of Tina's original thoughts:

In the first instance, there is actually no evidence that Tina's husband is pressuring her. Pete simply asked, "When do you want to start having children?" To pressure Tina, Pete would have to persist relentlessly, and be unwilling to back down from what he wants. In this example, he has only asked Tina "when?"

Next, while it may be true that Tina and Pete spoke about this very topic a few weeks ago, it is entirely possible that, in the excitement of the recent birth of his best friend's child, Pete may simply be raising the topic again. It is also possible that Pete's thoughts may have changed since their last discussion. Additionally, sometimes we think that we have made our point clear only to realize that our partner understood something very different from what we said. Even while they discussed the topic a few weeks ago, there is actually no evidence to suggest that Pete heard and understood exactly what Tina was trying to convey.

In Tina's third immediate thought, she makes the assumption that it will be so easy for Pete to have a kid. "Easy" is the pivotal word here since Tina's feelings of anger, irritation, and annoyance are based on this assumption. Unless Pete specifically says: "It's so easy to think about having kids," anything else is Tina's interpretation. If she hasn't already, Tina may ask Pete some additional questions, probing to find out exactly what he thinks about when he thinks about having kids. Therefore, there is no evidence that Tina's original thought is true.

Finally, Tina makes another assumption about Pete, telling herself that "his life won't change at all." Tina's absolutist way of thinking here gets her in trouble. When she critically examines her thoughts, she can see that this statement is not accurate. Tina actually knows that Pete's life will change—both of their lives will. Seeing her thoughts on paper helps Tina to realize that her all-or-nothing way of thinking creates strong negative emotions. Again, there is no actual evidence that Tina's original thought is true.

Challenging your thoughts forces you to examine their validity. Rarely will you feel overwhelmed by your emotions when your thoughts are accurate and valid.

Now, use "Where's the evidence?" as a prefix for the thoughts you recorded earlier.

Challenging my thoughts:

- "Where's the evidence .... "

_____

_____

- "Where's the evidence..... "

_____

_____

- "Where's the evidence.... "

_____

_____

- "Where's the evidence....."

_____

_____

Once you have created questions out of your thought statements, begin to answer these new questions. Where exactly, is the evidence that your thoughts are entirely accurate?

Challenging your thoughts with "Where's the evidence?" is often eye-opening. Rarely will you find evidential proof for your line of thinking. This is because many of your thoughts are not based in truth but rather in your perception of what is true. Since your thoughts are derived from your core beliefs, being consciously aware of your thoughts, feelings, and behaviors helps you to understand your current experience of "self."

Using "Where's the evidence?" is one strategy to help you change your thoughts.

A second strategy is to *look for alternative ways of thinking* about a particular situation. Record your thoughts as a way of examining the story that you have created in your mind. Next, examine your thoughts from the perspective of what you know to be true. Notice what immediately happens to your mood state. Being consciously aware of your thoughts in this particular moment enables you to accurately evaluate your initial perspective. As you critically examine your thoughts, you can remind yourself of an alternative way of viewing the situation rather than automatically accepting your "story" as truth.

An example of looking at a situation from a different (and more accurate) perspective might look like this:

You are speaking with some of your work colleagues. You notice that Sheila's behavior is different than usual. She was laughing at a joke someone made when you first walked over to the group, but you now notice that she is quiet and somewhat withdrawn. On a few different instances, you catch Sheila looking over at you—her brow furrowing and her lips pouting. You surmise that she is angry with you. You feel hurt and confused. You excuse yourself from the group a few moments later and retreat to your office cubicle, racking your brain to try and figure out what you did wrong.

In the above example, you may have decided that Sheila was upset or angry with you. In looking for an alternative possibility to your initial conclusion, you might decide to re-examine your perspective from a position of what you know to be true.

For instance,

Your question: "What do I know to be true?"
Your response: "Sheila didn't seem like herself today. I caught her looking at me with a frown on her face, but there could have been different reasons for that. I know that she has had a lot going on lately and has been debating whether or not to leave her boyfriend of three years."

Your *alternative* thought process to this situation: "Something definitely seems different with Sheila today. Rather than try and rack my brain to figure it out or blame myself for something that I could be completely wrong about, I'm going to go and ask her if everything is ok. She and I have always been able to talk openly."

Examining your thoughts closely and reframing them based on what you know to be true is vital if you want your feelings and reactions to be appropriate to a situation rather than over-reactive based on inaccurate perceptions and your biased version of the truth.

Changing Your Core Beliefs

Changing your core beliefs is the process for developing healthier, more positive ways of viewing yourself and the rest of the world. The question is: how do you go about changing the beliefs you've been holding onto for so long?

By challenging the core beliefs that limit you from being your best, you leave room to create new, alternative core beliefs—ones that are based in truth.

For the majority of my clients, uncovering a problematic core belief is done within the context of a therapy session using a methodology of guided questions that are determined by the progression of a client's response.

For the purpose of helping you self-identify one or more of your own core beliefs, I have provided a list of the most prevalent core beliefs for you to review. A core belief that resonates with you is one worth exploring further. Once you have identified a possible core belief, sit with it for a few days. Allow yourself to think about the way in which this particular core belief affects you. If it is one that is "accurate," you will be able to trace many examples of your daily thoughts back to it.

Identifying A Problematic Core Belief
Core beliefs that are problematic tend to resemble (or be a variation of) one or more of the following examples:

- "I'm not good enough" or "I'm not good enough at/as a ..."
- "I'm unlovable"
- "I'm stupid/not smart enough"

You identify a problematic core belief by being conscious of your pattern of thinking across situations in which you feel a series of discomforting or vulnerable emotions. Beliefs that are irrational cause you to remain stuck or immobile—and further reinforce a negative self-concept.

Examine a written list of your automatic thoughts in a reoccurring, problematic situation. Reoccurring situations are those in which you find yourself repeating certain behaviors that do not reflect how you would like to be. There is also a pattern of thinking in those situations that continues to replay itself in your mind. (e.g., reacting to feeling hurt by withdrawing [a behavior], reacting to thoughts that you "must be wrong or at fault" by apologizing and making concessions [behaviors] in order to appease your mate, or making snide or hurtful comments [a behavior] as a defense mechanism to feeling vulnerable or embarrassed.)

Examining your list of automatic thoughts in different situations helps identify a reoccurring theme. Reoccurring themes of "feeling not as good as" or "less than" point to a core belief of "not good enough" in some way. Reoccurring themes whereby you don't believe in yourself or make excuses for your actions often represent limited self-esteem and a core belief of "being unlovable" or "flawed" in some way. Doubting your ability or intellect even when you have evidence to prove the contrary is closely tied to a core belief of "not being smart enough."

As you identify a potential irrational core belief write it down and allow yourself time to process its relevance to the problematic thinking that you experience. It may be possible that you have identified two related core beliefs that simply need to be challenged independently of one another. Alternatively, you may need to make further adjustments to your core belief statement until it feels accurate for you.

Challenging Your Problematic Core Belief

Once you have identified an existing irrational core belief, you need to disprove it by challenging its accuracy.

Work with a single core belief at a time. Write it down on a blank piece of paper in front of you.

In order to challenge your core belief you need a good support team. Ask yourself the following questions: Who in my life can I trust to be truthful and honest with me? Whose opinion do I most value? (Some of the names you come up with will overlap.) Write the names of these people on your paper.

With your list of names in hand, ask yourself the next question. Which of these people would agree that this core belief is correct and accurate?

Because your problematic core belief is not evidence-based, it is quite likely that you will decide that the people whose opinion you value and trust would disagree with your belief.

If others who you trust to be honest with you disagree with your core belief, is it possible that your core belief is inaccurate?

If you answer "yes," the foundation of your core belief has just begun to crumble.

Creating an "Alternative" Core Belief

If important people in your life disagree with your original core belief, it's probably a good idea to consider rethinking what you have always believed to be true up until this moment. Challenging your limiting core belief allows you to make room for creating a more accurate and evidence-based core belief. You can repeat the same process for challenging any number of problematic core beliefs.

The most important criteria for a "new"
core belief is that it is based in truth.

Using similar language, devise an alternative core belief. Your new core belief needs to be based in what you believe to be true. Choose a core belief statement that you believe to be somewhat true (even if you only believe in it 5% at the moment). As you begin to strengthen your new core belief, you will believe in it more fully in no time.

Strengthening Your New Core Belief

Up to now, the core beliefs that you have carried with you for years has been reinforced time and again. To strengthen a new core belief, look for daily evidence that supports it. With your new core belief written at the top of a page in your journal, keep an ongoing record of evidence from each day that proves it to be valid. If you find it a challenge on some days, look for historical evidence. Each time you record a new piece of supporting evidence, your alternative core belief becomes stronger.

For example, if your limiting core belief is: "I do not deserve real happiness," perhaps your alternative core belief is: "I do deserve to feel happy and I have the power to create this for myself."

Evidence for your new core belief on a particular day might look like this:

- I made myself happy by choosing to take my car into work so I could enjoy being alone, rather than car pool with work colleagues.
- I felt happy in my decision to speak up on a work project that I am very much involved with. Letting others know my opinion is helpful for the overall success of the project.
- I decided to be proactive and called two friends in order to set up plans for this weekend. Now I can look forward to the weekend knowing that these are in place.
- I decided to treat myself and get take-out for dinner rather than cook.

Record every piece of evidence that supports your new core belief regardless of how small you deem it to be. Each time you record evidence, you strengthen your new core belief while simultaneously making your limiting core belief weaker.

Since it is likely that you have been living with your old core belief for several years, it will take some time before you begin to notice that it has much less of a hold on you. While it won't take years to unravel the belief you've been carrying around for so long, it's a good idea to continue collecting evidence for your alternative core belief for several months. Even when you notice that your daily thought patterns have changed significantly and are now based on your new core belief, its important to continue recording evidence. The daily evidence you collect ensures that your new core belief is well rooted, especially on days when you may still feel pangs of self-doubt. (Remember old habits die hard.) Additionally, you want to continue training yourself to look for evidence that supports your new belief system. This anchors a healthy way of being for future.

Choosing How You Want To Be

Regardless of your early environment, your life circumstances, and the varied subtle messages that you received from your parents and others when you were growing up, it is fundamentally your responsibility to change whatever holds you back from experiencing your life in a way that you most desire.

When I ask clients about their family history, it is in part to understand their operating template: their role model for a love relationship. It is also to gather information about how all of their earlier life experiences have affected who they currently are. In speaking about their initial "training ground," clients make important insights, regarding the origin of various belief systems, learned behaviors, specific personality traits, and the way in which they would like to be.

Even though you may not know how to go about making a specific change successfully, you do have the choice as to whether you continue to operate in the same way that you always have (perhaps at times, even miraculously expecting a different outcome), or whether you are willing to acknowledge that who you are is not exactly who you want to be. As a human being with the ability for critical thought, you have the capacity to choose how you are in life, as well as, who you are in your love relationship. Practicing conscious awareness is critical before you can expect to make any desired changes.

Just as you have begun to examine and challenge the core beliefs that are limiting and unsupportive to how you want to be, it's important that you also identify your positive core beliefs. These are also well established, although helpful to growing healthy self-esteem. Being kind, thoughtful, generous, outgoing, compassionate, good-natured, honest, caring, and truthful are only some of the many possible beliefs that you hold about yourself. Identify all of your positive core beliefs on a separate page in your journal, adding to these as you are reminded of additional traits.

As you work to replace limiting core beliefs with new, alternative ones, it's also important to consciously decide how you still want to be. Use your list of positive core beliefs to remind you of who you already are. Next, think about the qualities that you still want to adopt. For example, you may want to become more patient, more tolerant of others' differences, less judgmental, and consciously aware all of the time.

Record these qualities and traits in the form of a mantra. Memorize and repeat your mantra daily. Ensure that your mantra encompasses the way you want to be in the present rather than in future since you want to begin creating this now.

An example of a positive mantra, which your unconscious mind will hear and begin to support, may look like this:

"I am healthy, independent, and patient. I always seek to understand others and be accepting of their differences. I am consciously aware and often use this awareness to practice greater compassion and understanding of others."

You can create a mantra that includes all of the ways you want to change to become more. You can also create mantras for other areas of your life: e.g. being a loving, supportive partner, being an active and positive parent, being successful in your occupation, and so on.

As you remind yourself of all of your positive core beliefs, and rehearse your mantra, be patient as your levels of self-worth grow. Depending on the content of your mantra, it may take a year (or more) to actualize everything that you decide for yourself. Most importantly, you are doing all of the right things to create your ideal self.

Chapter Three

There is Purpose in Putting "You" First

The greater your devotion to self-worth and inner happiness, the greater likelihood that you will make relationship choices that honor what is most important for you.

Couples who knowingly remain in unhealthy relationships long past the point of being compatible on many levels, actually grow accustomed to the sense of disconnect that they feel from their authentic self, and from how they envisioned their life to be. Each day is filled with duties and responsibilities for a life that they didn't consciously choose. Whatever payoff keeps each member of the couple mired in relationship is small in comparison to how they feel every time they slow down long enough to hear their inner voice crying out in distress

If you allow yourself sufficient time to introspect on what aspects of yourself need to change, and what you ultimately need to do in order to be happy, you will figure out what needs fixing. The more difficult task is actually fixing what is wrong. You can have all of the right answers but if you are unwilling or afraid to do what work is necessary to get to happy, you stifle your own self-growth.

If you are fortunate enough to find a partner who supports your quest for personal growth—as you support theirs—you begin to realize the true purpose of a love relationship. With the right mate, you have support, comfort, and a mirror to reflect back to you how you *really* are—in order to see your self with different eyes. It is because of the unconditional love that you receive that you feel supported as you strive to grow, to change, and to become who you really want to be.

Just when I vowed to remain single indefinitely, to reassess my life's course, and to ensure that where I was headed was still where I wanted to go, a very interesting thing happened. The universe sent me an incredible someone who just happened to be in one of the few places in the world that I would be sure to notice. It was a single and unprompted two-minute conversation with a person that I had already known for the past year, that purposefully reminded me of what was really important in life. That conversation still resonates with me today.

Putting yourself first is not to be confused with taking care of your own needs at the expense of others. Rather, as you pay attention and honor your expression of self, you learn (even if this was not inherent in your upbringing) that your ability to give of yourself and to be your best self comes easiest when you attend to your own needs first.

What I encourage you to advocate for is "living in your truth." Being true to what you believe is best for you means that you will be more likely to choose a mate who has similar ideals. You will also choose based on your honest compatibility with another individual rather than how good they might appear to be "on paper" (e.g. their stated net worth, ability to provide for you, material possessions they have, and what they have told you they can offer).

When you haven't spent enough time figuring out what you need in order to be happy—and ensuring that you can provide yourself with those needs—it's more likely that you will find yourself in a relationship where few (if any) of your needs are being met. The appeal of being in a love relationship for the sake of not being alone, or being with the type of person that you are most physically attracted to (even when you know that the criteria that you have based your selection on is not ideal), can actually leave you feeling incredibly unhappy and alone.

Building healthy self-worth is fundamental to making the best choices as you go forward in your life. While a loving and supportive relationship can certainly contribute to your sense of self, you need to have the foundation in place. Self-esteem and self-worth are best developed initially in your family of origin. From there, it's up to you to continue that process.

Life Changing Moments

When you begin to spend time sitting quietly with your thoughts, your experience of your self changes. Rather than reacting to what is happening around you in your world, initiating quiet moments for reflection means that you can pull yourself out of the busy pace of "doing" and simply "be" for a while.

What happens in those moments of "quiet" is often life changing.

Experience a moment in your life that you have created. Simply sit somewhere where you can be alone for a few minutes. Ideally, you want to have complete quiet. (When you have complete quiet, it makes it so much easier to listen within.) And yes, to "find" quiet you may need to rise early in the morning before others wake up, find moments of alone time through the day, or be quiet after others have gone to sleep at night.

Using your breath as a place of focus, follow your inhalation into your body. Feel your chest and belly expand gently as you breathe in. As you exhale, feel your belly and chest return back inwards to your body. This is the simple process of tuning in to what your body is already doing when you are in a natural state of quiet and calm.

At first, simply focus on the inhalation and exhalation of your breath. As this becomes easier to do and as your attention can remain on your conscious breathing without being easily distracted, you can begin the next step.

Create a "blank mind," characterized by thoughts of "nothingness." The purpose of this is to learn how to intentionally empty your mind of all thoughts. (As easy as this may sound, it still requires practice.) Focus on your breathing and the experience of feeling your belly move in and out as you notice your mind slowly start to quiet. Visualize blackness (or any color that you may choose) as a way of creating a blank slate in your mind. As you continue to focus on the experience of conscious breathing, slowly notice the thoughts and ideas that begin to enter your mind.

Clearing your mind and then allowing thoughts to enter as you are in a state of calm is a purposeful way of connecting with your inner self. From here, you begin to receive information and ideas. Some of it may be related to your day-to-day life while other thoughts come in the form of images or solutions to problems or questions. If your mind becomes distracted or if you feel that your are directing your thoughts in the form of worry to something that has been troubling you, you may want to go back and clear your thoughts again as a means of clearing your focus for spontaneous ideas and information.

As you practice the skill of conscious breathing coupled with clear intentions – a clear direction for the outcome you want to achieve – you will be pleasantly surprised by all of the simple yet wonderful ideas and notions that come to you. Some may be as simple as the recognition of how you are feeling e.g. tired, calm, sad, peaceful; simple solutions to what you most need to do; or new thoughts and ideas providing guidance and direction or generating feelings of excitement and joy.

Conscious breathing in moments of "quiet" allows you to feel connected to your inner self, and to experience being grounded and centered. The ideas and thoughts that spontaneously enter your mind help provide guidance and direction. Your life changes as a result of this practice since you are now open to receiving information from your inner spirit, that you can hear most easily when your mind is fundamentally quiet.

As you maintain a commitment to this practice, it becomes easier to recognize the importance of creating moments that you intentionally carve out for yourself each day. Be open to the experience of quiet and of connecting with your inner self without preconceived notions of what should happen. In time, you will easily be able to elicit feelings of calm despite all of the activity and noise that continues to exist all around you.

Your Relationship With You

Your love relationships are a direct reflection of the relationship you have with yourself. With a healthy sense of self, you have greater clarity around what you want from a partner. You are able to thrive in your love relationship when you are happy with who you are and with the choices you have made for your life.

Without a strong sense of self and a clear direction and focus for your life, you inevitably experience greater challenges in your love relationship. Your insecurities intensify self-doubt, and it becomes easier to lose your identity, taking on the goals and aspirations of your partner rather than developing your own. While lacking a strong sense of self doesn't impede most people from being in a love relationship, the choices that you make, and the level of honesty and self-worth that you operate from, is compromised.

Your self-effacing and self-critical thoughts show up in all of your love relationships. The same goes for your ability to have patience, determination, commitment, and self-discipline. If you are quick to criticize and berate yourself for self-perceived lapses in what you deem acceptable, how quick are you to judge your mate based on the high expectations that you hold? How easy will it be to offer patience and understanding to your loved one if you are continually impatient and unforgiving of yourself? The way in which you treat your partner is a direct reflection of how you treat your self.

- To have a good relationship with your self requires that you have made the effort to know and understand who you are, and that you remain honest and accepting of yourself, even as you may consciously work on becoming more.
- To have a healthy relationship with your self means that you have self-respect and dignity even as you may not always act in ways that are in line with how you would like to be. To know how you would like to behave with others and to work towards becoming the best that you can be (even when you are not always successful in this) means that you continue to evolve. To uphold a personal commitment to always asking more of yourself means that your self-worth and self-esteem continue to grow.
- To have a loving relationship with your self means that you choose your inner dialogue carefully. You speak to yourself

with kind and compassionate words, knowing that your unconscious mind is always listening. You acknowledge and embrace the responsibility of self-love.

Unlike much of the traditional literature on love relationships, which primarily focused on helping couples to improve their relationship dynamics and interactions, this book underscores the magnitude of what can be accomplished when you strive to focus on improving your self first. When both members of a couple remain committed to their personal growth and self-fulfillment, they are unquestionably far more content and happy with who they are, and with their life. Consequentially, this happiness and inner fulfillment, while it requires ongoing attention and effort to uphold, becomes the underlying basis for both members of a couple to effortlessly share of themselves, largely because they can do so more easily when they have already taken care of their individual needs.

Looking at Lena, you would assume that she had it all together. Married to Anthony, a successful entrepreneur, and mother of three children all under the age of five, Lena was petite in stature and very attractive. Even as a busy mom, she always looked impeccable, with a great sense of style. From the outside looking in, Lena was demure, polite, and intelligent. One would think that she had it all.

When Lena first came to see me, she spoke mostly about her marriage. Together for nine years, Lena and Anthony had navigated through years of difficult tension between his parents and her, the financial stress of Anthony's business in its early years, and more recently a love relationship that had lost its spark. Lena described how she and Anthony now fought constantly and had a virtually non-existent sex life.

Over the course of the next few months, I saw Lena for individual sessions, as well as together with Anthony. On two occasions, Anthony came in to talk about his own frustrations with Lena's behavior and his growing concern for a bleak future if nothing changed.

Lena admitted that one of the main problems was her uncontrollable rage. Even though she had good intentions to be the best mother and wife, Lena couldn't seem to handle the stress and frustrations that went along with being a stay-at-home mom. Anthony reported that he would arrive at the front door to hear his wife yelling at the top of her lungs. He would walk into the house to find one or more of the children crying while Lena would be ranting. Often the anger would then be redirected at Anthony who typically would fight back with heavy sarcasm. In Anthony's mind, Lena's temper was uncontrollable.

Lena admitted that she was unhappy with her life, and yet she believed that her being home full-time was ultimately the best thing for their young children. Lena was determined to raise her kids without day care or a nanny, even though she and Anthony could easily have afforded them. Having barely survived an earlier history of intense conflict with her in-laws, Lena could not entrust them to take "proper" care of her children. In trying to maintain control in what felt like constant chaos, Lena had lost her self. She had also lost the ability to control her raging emotions.

While Lena truly wanted to be the best mother and wife possible, she treated everyone around her, her kids included, in a way that (literally) screamed anger. Ultimately, Lena was most angry with herself. While on the surface it appeared that she had things under control, Lena's actions spoke volumes. Lena was deeply frustrated with her life and yet continued to be governed by the self-limiting choices that she had created. While Lena maintained her parental authority by refusing to allow anyone else (including Anthony) a voice in how the children were being raised, she had ultimately lost control over her own life and who she had become.

While you may not always be able to figure everything out before launching into a love relationship, your relationship with your self continues to be the most important one that you foster. Even as you work at building a healthy love relationship, you also need to honor your relationship with your self.

Below are some key questions to reflect upon as you think about the kind of relationship you currently have with your self. Please use a notebook to record your answers and to review and add additional thoughts and ideas.

Your Relationship With You

1. Who am I?
SUGGESTION: Use key words to describe the likes, dislikes, beliefs, values, and character traits that comprise the person you believe you are.

_____

_____

_____

_____

2. What aspects of myself do I most like / admire?
What aspects of myself do I dislike / want to be different?
SUGGESTION: Include personality traits as well as aspects of your physical, intellectual, and emotional self.

_____

_____

_____

_____

3. What are my biggest stumbling blocks to becoming who I want to be?

_____

_____

_____

_____

4. What behaviors tell me that I love and honor myself?

_____

_____

_____

_____

When you enter into a love relationship, you are hopeful, excited, and captivated by the strong positive feelings that you experience, including those that you feel and receive from your partner. There is an underlying expectation that the person who loves you will always provide all of the incredible things (respect, support, love, attention, affection) that continue to make you happy.

What you tend to forget is that you are also expected to provide all of these same elements and even to intuit what your partner needs without them always having to ask. (All of this is unspoken, of course, since our expectations are rarely laid out as logically and clearly as we might think them in our minds.)

Then something very interesting starts to happen. You realize that your partner is not always able to provide what you need. They start to let you down (remember, you have put expectations on them without ever telling them so), disappoint you, even fail you at times. You begin to think that their love for you has somehow changed when in fact it is simply that they also have their own insecurities, vulnerabilities, flaws, and fears to work through.

At some point, after the initial honeymoon stage of getting to know each other and showing all of your best self, you relax a little. When you allow yourself a chance to exhale, you redirect some of your energy and attention to taking care of your own needs. For example, you now need to put extra effort into your career if you want that promotion to happen; you may worry about how to manage your boss's expectations since he always demands more than what you feel is reasonable; you are asked to step in and deal with the ongoing conflict between your parents, as well as the many other life events that require your attention every day. When you let go (even a little) of the intensity of what you were previously giving to your love relationship, you are left with the reality of what is.

Lena admitted that she had not been completely truthful with herself (nor with Anthony) about how she wanted her life to unfold. Aware of the social mores of her culture and the importance placed on having a family, Lena was caught between what she really wanted to do and the obligations she was raised to adopt. Lena confessed that hadn't really wanted to start a family so soon—if, perhaps, at all. Knowing that Anthony deeply wanted children, she felt obliged to become a mother thinking that she would have his undivided emotional support. Now that her life was so different from what she originally imagined, Lena felt resentful toward Anthony and the children. As primary caregiver, she didn't feel intellectually stimulated being at home all day. Lena's ideal image of motherhood—based on her memories of her own mother as calm, loving, organized, and perfect—had been completely shattered after the birth of her first child. Looking back, she admitted that she had no idea how her life had become what it was.

For Lena to feel happy again meant taking the first step to verbalize what she truthfully felt. In sharing with Anthony some of her most intimate thoughts and feelings, Lena was surprised by his understanding and support. After some further soul searching and talks with Anthony, Lena landed a great part-time job as an interior designer with a local firm. Doing so meant that she had to let go of some of the control she sought over childcare. Anthony and Lena decided to use a professional daycare for two of the three days Lena worked outside the home. They compromised letting both sets of grandparents take turns caring for their children on the third day Lena worked each week

In a healthy love relationship, you and your partner easily sustain attention and focus on your individual lives. You recognize and know the importance of making yourself happy, independent of (but not exclusive to) your love relationship.

Without conscious awareness that they are doing so, many people ultimately look to their love relationship to nurture and fulfill most of their emotional needs. They expect to be loved, taken care of, appreciated, and valued. They choose a partner because they believe that, in some way, their partner will allow them to feel complete. Of course, they do not anticipate what actually follows.

Zoe and John walked into my office in quiet solitude. John had called only days earlier, determined to get an appointment as quickly as possible. The couple explained that they had come for counseling in a desperate last attempt to help them save their relationship. Married seven months, the couple had separated earlier that week.

As newlyweds, John and Zoe appeared to have few of the typical external stresses of most young couples. Living in a beautiful four-bedroom house that they owned outright, both Zoe and John had full-time jobs and little in the way of monthly expenses. They described sharing similar cultural backgrounds and strong traditional customs governing the expectations for how both genders behaved in a marriage.

What became resoundingly clear as the session progressed, however, was the degree of anger and resentment that each felt toward the other. Listening carefully to their escalating voices trading accusations and blame, I could see that Zoe had given away all of her power. She had, in fact, entered into this relationship without a voice. Based on the traditional marital roles both were exposed to growing up, Zoe allowed John to make most of the decisions in the relationship, and to direct much of what the couple did together. Naturally, Zoe was unhappy, realizing she wasn't getting what she needed. Instead of figuring out what was right for her and acting on it, Zoe went along with all that John decided—quietly at first, and then more openly because she was outraged at the lack of equality and fairness. John had been taught that it was his role as a husband to take charge of the couple's life. He couldn't understand why Zoe, in turn, was so ungrateful and angry.

Without the skills to identify and acknowledge her own needs, Zoe relied on John to somehow know how to make her happy. In giving up so much of her personal power by allowing John to make the majority of decisions in the relationship, Zoe was abdicating her right to be happy without even realizing that her personal happiness had to come from within. Since Zoe blamed John for everything that went wrong, he easily became the target of all of her anger. As Zoe's anger and criticism toward John escalated, he began fighting back with increasing aggression. It was a battle that had no ending.

Without believing that she had the final say in her life, Zoe would continue to be miserable. Without establishing a healthy relationship with herself, Zoe would continue to expect that others should just know what would make her happy—and then be terribly disappointed when she wasn't.

Unfortunately, that single visit to my office was the only time I saw John and Zoe as a couple. Giving them both some immediate directives to work on as well as an honest perspective on what they both needed to do was only a starting place. As a final attempt at saving a love relationship, sometimes therapy comes too late. It would be more than a year later when I bumped into Zoe, single, happy, and grateful that she had ended her relationship. Zoe was kind enough to thank me for validating what she knew deep down was the right thing. She was now in the process of figuring out her needs and being responsible for her own happiness. She also reassured me that she was rethinking her role for future love relationships.

Each person automatically brings all of their previous "life baggage" with them each time they begin a new relationship. In fact, your "life baggage" continues metaphorically to take up space in your life if you never bother to empty it. The larger the pile of baggage, the more you are symbolically (and sometimes physically) weighed down, making it very difficult for you to be happy and to be able to give of yourself in relationship.

Instead, who you are becomes clouded by the inevitable heartaches and wounds of your previous relationships, as well as your experiences from childhood in your family of origin.

When you don't accept full responsibility for your personal happiness, you continue to find excuses, blame others, and deny your own part in creating the situations that leave you feeling troubled and unhappy. Ultimately, the place you need to go first is within yourself.

Beginning With "Happy"

It is much easier to reveal your true self when you feel content and happy. However, no matter how hard you try, it's pretty difficult to achieve a constant state of happiness during every waking moment. Your first step, therefore, is to be able to feel a sense of authentic happiness from within. The key to tapping into your innate capacity for happiness begins with being fully honest with yourself. You then need to live in that honesty (both inwardly and when expressing your thoughts and feelings to others). By living in a place of complete and total honesty you begin to create a life that allows you to feel truly happy—all of the time.

By acting on your honest thoughts and feelings, you begin to build a world that is based on your truth. I say "your" truth because each of us has a different background and set of life experiences that contributes to (and affects) what we know will be right and best for ourselves. Unfortunately, few people spend the time to figure out what they truly need in order to be happy. Often because to do so means making some tough decisions, the majority of people carry on with their lives without taking an honest reprieve to determine and then fix the source of their unhappiness.

The majority of people have been socialized to do for others, to be self-sacrificing, and to make decisions out of guilt rather than inner desire and purpose. The end result means living behind a façade. Life becomes a series of events based on what we think we should do, rather than what we really want to be doing. We build a life around what we think is expected of us, and what we perceive will make other people happy without ever following that inner voice that is screaming "no, No, NO!"

When you don't listen to your inner voice—your truth—speaking to you, you are left with feelings of anxiety, sadness, emptiness, anger, resentment, fear, and of course, ultimate unhappiness.

Because you feel unhappy (even if you don't articulate it as unhappiness), you look to other people and things to fill that void. You become highly skilled at distracting yourself from your life because it's the distractions that make you feel slightly better in that moment. Your relationships with those closest to you become heavily strained because you live in a place of inner turmoil and angst that shows, repeatedly.

You begin looking for a "quick fix" because doing what would be required to genuinely make you happy would mean changing careers, ending your current relationship, selling your beautiful home, living on a drastically reduced income, or any combination of these. Any of these possibilities seem daunting, which is why you remain immobilized (even though on some level you know that several of these are what you ultimately need to do to get to happy). Let's face it: it's easier to live in your ever-so-familiar existence even if you are miserable (stuck, trapped, or suffocated) because the unknown factor that goes with making these life changes seems far scarier.

And yet there should be some sort of disclaimer for how your unconscious mind operates. As you quietly yearn for a change in your reality, your unconscious mind listens. Your thoughts and ideals for what you would like to see begin influencing your behaviors, moving you, even without full consciousness, in the direction of the reality you want to create.

During our first session, Lawrence described his wife's self-deprecating pattern as the result of her overall unhappiness. Lawrence depicted a pattern in which Patricia would become silent when something bothered her. He explained how frustrating it was to continually probe, often to no avail, to find out what was wrong. He surmised that Patricia felt as though she had put her own life on hold, having been the primary caregiver for their four children. Patricia occasionally spoke of a career designing hand-made jewelry but did little to realize this dream much to her husband's frustration. Lawrence was a powerhouse at work and a "doer." He indicated that he continued to support and encourage Patricia to create a business out of her incredible talent, even while he noted that she did little beyond talk about her dream.

In the two years before Lawrence came to see me, Patricia had the equivalent of a mid-life crisis. She went on extravagant shopping sprees, spending vast amounts of her husband's money, began extensive interior decorating projects in their summer home, and had a series of personal cosmetic procedures with the intention of looking more youthful. Patricia dressed provocatively and (as Lawrence described) "more like her teenage daughter than a woman in her early 50s." Lawrence also noted that she began "disappearing" for hours at a time leaving her family with no means of contacting her.

Instead of being honest with herself about what was making her unhappy, Patricia's life had spun out of control. She had started an intense affair with a much younger man who happened to be one of her husband's commercial real estate agents.

While Patricia had initially felt alive and excited, the affair quickly became a messy disaster. When he initially came to see me, Lawrence and his teenage children were living in the family home while Patricia had moved into a condo in the city. Her affair quickly died as it became increasingly apparent to Patricia that her lover never had any serious intentions of maintaining any kind of lasting relationship with her. While Lawrence and Patricia had several unresolved issues in their relationship long before Patricia's affair, Lawrence was now seeking my help to overcome his feelings of betrayal and anger. He had begun to think about how his actions and behaviors had contributed to Patricia's growing level of unhappiness over the years. These included Lawrence's long work days and extended travel, which had left Patricia to raise their four kids largely by herself, his constant criticism of her parenting style and the decisions that she made, and his inability to be "present" even when he was home. Lawrence confessed that he did want to work things out and was hoping that Patricia would want the same.

Patricia's lack of honesty in acknowledging the real problem— her own feelings of unhappiness—meant that she had moved even further away from her truth and from finding the solution. By stepping into another relationship, however casual or harmless she thought it would be, Patricia inevitably created more inauthenticity in her life. In her efforts to avoid her current state of unhappiness, Patricia created a temporary "quick fix" in order to feel better. Unfortunately, her actions hurt several others along the way.

If you are unhappy, it doesn't have to be another person that you search for. Many people continue in a prolonged state of unhappiness because of what their life affords them. They purchase the things that temporarily provide them with relief from their unhappy lives. They escape their lives (even for only a short while) by traveling with their work, or taking on additional projects that allow them to remain largely preoccupied. They confuse work success, their children's success, or their socioeconomic status with authentic happiness because these things (work, children, money) allow them moments of personal satisfaction, monetary reinforcement, and status.

In other cases, escape comes in the illusionary form of what we call "moving forward with life." Becoming pregnant, buying a new house, leasing a new car, changing jobs are all attempts to convince ourselves that a child (or another child!), a bigger house, a better car, or a new job will make us happy. We tell ourselves that our relationship will miraculously improve when we have a new something that will in some way complete us. Once what we have inserted into our life becomes yet another thing that we have to attend to at the expense of attention to our self, we begin to feel the impending sense of unhappiness take hold again.

Beginning within for your state of happiness means a full assessment of your life and how you are currently living it. Being honest with yourself is the critical starting point for creating happiness. When you make choices that are not in line with what creates authentic happiness, you can be assured that you have just taken one more detour from "getting to happy." The best question to ask yourself to make sure that your path is the right one for you is: "Will this _____ make me happy? What will make me happiest at this moment?" Making honest choices even if they differ from others around you means that you follow a life course that is right for you. Doing so makes it so much easier than having to consider a number of major life changes later on.

Fortunately, Lawrence and Patricia were able to come together and begin an open and honest dialogue. Patricia began individual therapy as a means of understanding the underlying causes of her unhappiness. Remaining committed to the process Patricia was able to figure out what she needed to do for her self to get to happy. With the support of her family and therapist, Patricia began to heal as she forgave herself, and moved in the direction of what *she* needed in order to be happy and fulfilled.

Lawrence learned to listen to Patricia and be a gentle supporter for her. He worked hard to forgive her as well as accept the person that she is (acknowledging that Patricia was different from him, but that, that was alright). Lawrence began to focus on making personal changes of his own, correcting the behaviors that had been bothering him for some time. Patricia and Lawrence have since started living together again and have made significant changes in who they are with each other as a result of working on their individual happiness.

Your personal happiness comes from investing time and energy in your self. Regardless of where you are in your life (including whether or not you feel able to make any needed changes), love yourself enough to begin spending what I call "alone time." Even if you are not prepared to transform how you live your life right now, learn how to pay attention to your self and your own needs. This will help you to make decisions and choices that will bring you moments of happiness even while you begin changing the bigger areas of your life.

The greater your devotion to self-worth and inner happiness, the greater likelihood you will make relationship choices that honor what is most important and right for you. When you begin from a place of "happiness," you are far less likely to get caught up in a life that was never what you wanted. Beginning from a place of happiness allows you to be honest with yourself about what you look for in an ideal mate. Being self-aware, introspective and directive of your own thoughts, feelings, and behaviors, means that you can choose an ideal partner who can compliment who you are.

Rethinking Cultural Norms

There are many stereotypical behaviors that show up for both men and women in relationships. We tend to easily adopt "culturally accepted" mores for how we live in relationship without really asking the question: What is right for me?

One of the most widespread expectations for individuals in relationship is the notion of thinking as a couple. The infamous "we" takes over everyday language making life a product of the cumulative effort of two people, rather than of two individuals in a love relationship.

Historically (and certainly prior to the start of the feminist movement), women were far more likely to express themselves as a "we" during dating and upon marriage. Traditional societal mores dictated that a woman's role in a love relationship was largely tied up in activities that were centered around home life and rearing a family. Today, women immigrating from countries where they have been taught to believe that, once married, their husband is the decision-maker of the household still struggle with maintaining a strong sense of their individual self as they may still hold some of the traditional views of motherhood, domestic chores, and career.

In examining traditional roles within a love relationship, we see value placed on a man's duties and responsibilities in providing for his family. Male self-worth is modeled on success in the workplace, power, and on monetary gains. Even as much as we expect responsibilities and effort to be shared equally, many existing love relationships still follow traditional and convenient patterns based on pre-existing gender roles from earlier times.

On a much more subtle level, women and men think differently when in a love relationship. You and your partner might separately answer the following questions and then compare notes to illustrate just how different your thoughts and expectations are about your respective roles while in relationship together.

Relationship Encounter: "Identifying Expectations"

Deconstruct the various socially ascribed roles between men and women by asking the following questions:

How does who you are change once you begin a love relationship?

_____

_____

_____

_____

What are your expectations of your partner (and of yourself) now that you are a couple?

_____

_____

_____

_____

What have you compromised, or have chosen to do differently, now that you are in a relationship?

_____

_____

What are your individual roles now that you are in relationship together? What roles have each of you automatically assumed that you may want to reconsider?

_____

_____

_____

_____

Does your "couple" relationship come at the expense of aspects of who you are as individuals?

_____

_____

_____

_____

I recently spoke with my close friend, Meghan, about some of the frustrations she was experiencing in her four-year relationship. A talented artist, Meghan was feeling angry and defeated as she spoke about Jared, her boyfriend, with whom she had lived for three years. Jared was an engineer who came from a family of very traditional, gender-specific roles. Jared's father was a mechanic who never assisted with domestic chores while Jared's mother stopped working outside the home once her children were born. Even though Jared did help to clean the apartment and loved to cook, Meghan still experienced a painful unbalance in the chores that she was left to do.

As I began to ask some pointed questions, Meghan admitted that Jared was far more tolerant of their living conditions than she was. Meghan would typically do the majority of the laundry (most of which she described as belonging to Jared), keep the kitchen tidy, and clean the apartment, spurred by her own self-confessed intolerance of mess. While she liked her environment to be extremely neat, especially as she worked primarily out of her home studio, Meghan recognized that if she was going to give up feeling frustrated and resentful, she first needed to learn how to "let go" of wanting everything to be perfect.

In any love relationship, there may be gender-specific norms that (however quietly) women adopt as ways of being. Often this translates into a desire to make everything work well, even if it means initiating what is perceived as a greater amount of effort and attention into day-to-day activities. The problem with adopting gender-specific behaviors (if we can call them that) lies in teaching our partners that this is what we want. If we were to take a close look at all of the things that we do in a relationship because of what we have been socialized to do them, we actually might start making different decisions.

Societal, cultural, and religious norms and expectations make it very easy for us to fall into certain roles in relationships. What we need to remember is that we teach others how to treat us. Meghan taught Jared that it was perfectly acceptable to let her do more of the chores since she simply did them. While Jared would certainly contribute, he would do so based on his level of tolerance. Since Meghan and Jared had very different standards for what was acceptable in their apartment, and since Jared didn't believe in tidying up daily, they were at a huge impasse.

Furthermore, Jared really had no idea why Meghan was so angry with him. He simply didn't think that the apartment looked messy and he would often appease Meghan by responding "yes" to all of her cleaning demands, even when he would not get around to completing all of them. When Meghan confided in me, she was literally at an emotional breaking point. The unbalanced division of chores and the value she placed in keeping her surroundings neat was affecting her ability as an artist to do her work.

On a pragmatic level, it is easiest to discuss ground rules for the division of labor almost immediately when two people begin living together. By establishing upfront the expectations each person has for how tasks and chores will be divided in the relationship, you can avoid a lot of problems later

If norms have already been established for how things are done—usually through a process of some communication, coupled with a customary routine that is often based on socialized expectations—it is far more challenging to begin deconstructing expectations and rules for how things ought to be.

Since Meghan came to me in desperation, I recommended a very specific course of action, a program that may seem unconventional to most, but if a whole new pattern of being was necessary, then a completely different system of operating expectations was in order. I suggested that if Meghan was to be able to "let go" of some of her need to have everything a certain way (something she was used to, having lived for many years on her own), she needed to take care of her own chores. This meant doing her own laundry, making her own lunch, and cooking for herself since, unlike Jared, Meghan's work dictated that she didn't have the same eating schedule.

Simultaneously, I encouraged Meghan to carve out her studio as her personal "sanctuary." She was allowed to keep her studio as neat and as organized as she needed it to be to feel comfortable, while letting go of the need to keep the whole apartment the same way. She would not stop doing things that she wanted to do for Jared, but she would stop cleaning up after him and doing his share of the chores out of her own need to "be tidy."

Meghan was also to stop demanding that Jared do more around the apartment. The expectation was that Meghan would simply concentrate more of her time and energy on her work as an artist and do her half of the domestic duties. With heartfelt communication, Jared would hopefully begin to "learn" that his share of responsibilities (which were no longer being done for him), were up to him. Slowly, Jared would be able to take his own initiative to do what would be considered his share.

What do you think was the outcome?

When Meghan slowly gave up some of her need to impose her standards for cleaning and household chores on Jared, she began to notice some interesting changes. To her surprise, Jared did not complain that Meghan was doing less work in the apartment. Jared even began initiating household chores and followed them through to completion even when Meghan no longer jumped in to help.

Secondly, Jared saw Meghan putting a lot more time into her work and slowly started to take care of his own laundry, dishes and his share of tidying the apartment on a slightly different time line. To Meghan's delight, Jared began pitching in to help on more of a daily basis, rather than when things became intolerably messy.

With some discipline and practice, Meghan admitted that she had learned how to let go of her compulsive need to have everything just so all of the time. Freeing up a great deal of time to focus on her own career meant that she was able to get so much more accomplished—and she no longer felt resentful towards Jared.

When you begin to reassess what it is that you are doing in your relationship that is not serving your highest good—that which makes you inwardly happy—then it becomes critical to question the expectations you hold of yourself and of the way you have defined your roles within your love relationship. In your own self-evaluation, you will undoubtedly need to come back to self-honesty, based on what is right and best for you. This is not at the expense of caring for your loved one, but it is, however, about remembering that you alone are responsible for your own happiness.

Pay attention to the socially ascribed roles that you have chosen to reinforce in your love relationship. To expect that your partner will automatically adopt your beliefs for how things should be in a relationship will only provoke feelings of frustration and discontent. To ascribe to a particular methodology or way of being purely to please your partner or to carry out certain predetermined roles suggests that you have indeed lost some of your self.

The Search For Self

The majority of your adolescent years are spent in a state of exploration and self-discovery. Your self-image (the internal picture you have of yourself) and self-concept (how you think about yourself), although largely formulated by this time, continue to subtly transform as you embrace challenges and strive to achieve. In experiencing relationships with family, peers, and most importantly with those you love, your sense of self is most visibly reflected back to you.

Loving another human being doesn't preclude you from being who you are. Part of what you are able to learn from being in a love relationship is how to retain your identity—your sense of self—even as you integrate your life with another person.

To have a healthy sense of self is to know yourself intimately and to remain true to the best parts of what you discover. As you set out to consciously develop your sense of self, take time to think carefully about what you believe to be right for you, despite what external pressures you may feel. Staying true to what you innately experience as authentic for you takes courage. It means standing your ground, at times without the full support of others, in order to honor your spirit and to experience your self fully.

Your earliest relationships have helped shape who you are, and yet, they certainly don't define you. Most importantly, your earlier relationships teach you valuable life lessons and set the stage for continued growth and self-awareness. They are instrumental in teaching you something of value if you look close enough.

Having a healthy sense of self when you enter into a relationship means that you are more likely to be able to navigate through the difficult emotions that surface when aspects of your relationship are not going smoothly. Being confident in who you are means that you can be in relationship with someone who has different opinions on some—not all—topics and not be swayed by them. Your ultimate love relationship will always be with someone who shares similar values, beliefs, and views of the world.

One of the great purposes of living is in the advancement of the self. You advance or develop your self through learning, growing, and becoming a more complete and evolved human being. Toward this end, you have the ability to learn from your hardships and mistakes, to educate yourself through your life experiences, and to choose to want to become a better person. You recognize that you are on your own individual life journey as a result of needing to heal your earlier wounds, as well as to be able to give back to the world through who you are and what you do with your life. To have spent the time and effort in evolving and knowing your self means that you know how to give of yourself in relationship with another.

One of the major revelations for couples is the importance of working on the individual self as an integral and inescapable part of improving the relationship. In therapy, personal goals are concurrently addressed within the context of those specific to the couple relationship. Having clients address their individual issues makes it possible to readily understand what compromises their sense of personal happiness.

In a love relationship, you need to be willing to continue building your own sense of self, independently of how you experience yourself with your mate. Upon completing their formal education, most people don't think about continuing some form of personal development. But if neither member of a couple has invested thoughtful effort in identifying and pursuing their individual needs (and experiencing what it feels like to be self-sufficient in the creation of their personal happiness), they are likely to struggle to maintain their senses of self.

Sam and Elenya seemed to have a romantic and idyllic courtship. They were both born in Russia and dated for six months prior to being married. At the time, Elenya was 15 and Sam was 23. Even after immigrating to North America, their traditional beliefs meant that Sam worked 12-15 hour days running his own business, to support his family and his parents back home, while Elenya maintained a conventional role within the home raising their three children.

As Elenya's sons grew up and became independent young adults, she began to have more time for herself. Elenya began working full time—her first job ever—and enjoyed the freedom and independence that came with earning her own money. Elenya's self-esteem grew as she became more confident in her abilities, and experienced many positive successes at work. Slowly, Elenya's life began to include frequent social outings with her female friends, some of whom were separated and divorced. Since Sam worked long hours, he was content to be at home and to look after their sons while Elenya and her friends would go out several times a week.

Elenya explained that perhaps for the first time in her life, she was "having fun." Giving birth to her first child at age 18, Elenya was only now beginning to explore who she was, including her physical attractiveness and sexuality. While Sam had dated several women prior to meeting Elenya, he was her first and only love. Coupled with the enormous changes in her life that followed after having three children, Elenya had never really established her own sense of self apart from her role as wife and mother.

Now, at age 34 and with a few more freedoms, Elenya had picked up where she had left off years earlier. With so many new experiences in her life, Elenya began to realize all that she missed out on by getting married so young. The problem, as Elenya quietly admitted, was that she was caught up in the newfound attention of other men, and had begun a secret affair.

As Elenya's life offered more freedoms and experiences, she yearned to do all of the things that she felt she had missed out on.

She also felt a growing resentment toward her children, her husband, and even her parents whom she blamed for encouraging her to get married at a time when all she really wanted to do was enjoy her adolescence. Elenya was now struggling to increase her self-esteem and self-confidence while she tried to figure out what would make her happy.

For both Sam and Elenya, having to face their truth was extremely difficult. Sam openly acknowledged that he had done little to help build Elenya's self-esteem throughout their relationship. Instead he frequently told Elenya that she "was stupid" and "would never make it on her own." Now, Sam admitted that he felt jealous at times to see how successful Elenya had become. With two promotions behind her, she was working on projects that she never thought she could. Even without formal training and education, Eleyna's sharp intelligence made it easy for her to learn quickly. Sam recognized that his heartfelt praise for his wife and her accomplishments was too little, too late. As much as he was determined to save their marriage, Sam realized that he had mistreated Elenya for a long time. He had actually contributed to her low self-worth and self-esteem.

When I last worked with Elenya and Sam, they were going to continue to heal their relationship. Elenya had ended her affair and was working to rebuild trust with Sam. Sam began to genuinely encourage and support Elenya's career, as well as her decision to pursue a college degree part-time. Both recognized the importance of carving out quality time to spend together as a couple, and to appreciate each other's need for individual growth and fulfillment.

Your role in your relationship with your significant other, your children, even your extended family (if you are not careful), can become an incredible distraction from focusing on your self. By investing your time and energy in fulfilling the needs of your spouse, your children, and even your aging parents—to the exclusion of your own needs—you are left feeling empty inside.

Tangentially, we sometimes combat the often unconscious feeling of emptiness that starts to creep up with tasks such as shopping, eating, working, excessive exercise, Internet surfing, spending time with friends...almost any task that allows us some immediate gratification, however short-lived it may be.

And yet, if you actually slow down long enough to pay attention to how you came to be feeling empty or lost inside, you might feel a sense of resentment, regret, or indignation. You wonder "How did this happen?" when in fact all that you ever needed to do was pay greater attention to your own needs. Once you clearly identify the fundamental needs that support your sense of self (some of which may include: feeling confident and more self-assured in your career objectives, having more confidence in your physical appearance, positive activities and interests that you enjoy, accomplishing long-standing goals, and so on) you are more likely to address and take care of those needs. You begin to pay attention to those areas of your life that matter most. You are more willing to do something about the areas you identified because to do so means that you will be happier as a result.

A healthy love relationship is founded on mutual respect and support. When each person in the couple can enjoy the rich experience of their individual life—and by that I mean their own interests, career, activities, and friends—they can come home at the end of each day and contribute to the relationship by sharing of their self. When you choose to live your life in a way that allows you to feel a sense of fulfillment, you are then able to share that intrinsic happiness with your partner. If both members of a couple live this way, it becomes easy to experience a mutually supportive and loving relationship.

The basic message that I relay to all of my couple clients is to simultaneously work on feeling good about their individual selves even as they work on fostering a healthy and respectful relationship with each other. If you are unhappy with aspects of your self, this will consistently affect how you are in your relationship. Without a good sense of self, all of the smaller day-to-day issues are harder to navigate through. Resolving conflict and communicating your inner thoughts and feelings (without being mired in ego and fear) becomes far more challenging when you feel less confident (and happy) in who you are.

Because your sense of self continues to develop throughout your life, beginning as early as infancy but most substantially during pre-adolescence and throughout the decade of your teens and twenties, it's important to consistently invest time and effort in evolving who your self is. Your love relationships, and the people you choose to be in a relationship with are infinitely important in helping you to assess and reassess what is important to you.

Alone Time—What a Concept!

We live in a society where the focus is on doing rather than being. We continue to be evaluated on our performance when performance is based on results of accomplishment. Far less value is attached to reflective thinking, introspection, or quiet time spent alone. In fact, we have become so skilled at filling every waking moment of our day with activities and action that it is no wonder that we have grown more and more detached from our self, and as a result, from what we need in order to be happy.

When we make time to be quiet and alone with our thoughts it gives our conscious mind a chance to de-stress. As we become quiet—especially if we can sit with our eyes closed and eliminate external stimuli—we can pay attention to our breathing and re-connect with what we are feeling in our bodies. We learn how to pay attention to all of the signals and messages that our bodies constantly send us. Once we begin to practice greater self-awareness, it becomes possible to identify all that we need.

Creating quiet alone time may be a challenge at first. It is very difficult to actually sit still and do nothing but breathe and be with yourself, in part because your brain continues to be highly active. You train your mind to slow down and become quiet, largely from using your breathing in quiet meditation.

As a society, we've actually become quite good at not thinking. We've mastered the art of keeping busy (whether we realize it or not) largely as a way of distracting ourselves from a plethora of thoughts and uncomfortable feelings (e.g. anxiety, sadness, anger, and emotional pain). This is a good example of how our thoughts (especially as they go unmonitored most of the time) create what seem like uncontrollable feelings. To avoid feeling a certain way, we often react by keeping busy, not always realizing that our thoughts don't ever really go away.

And yet, if you can stay committed to the practice of sitting quietly with your self, interesting and amazing things begin to happen. You notice that you are able to focus strictly on your breathing for longer periods of time. You become better at allowing thoughts to enter your mind, observing them but letting them be rather than going with the urge to act on them. You begin to reconnect sooner to your physical self, noticing how your breathing can help you to feel calm or even relaxed. You become more disciplined in the art of self-awareness, connecting to your self on a core level.

Most of us have never really learned the inherent value of spending time alone, reflecting, meditating, visualizing, and of course being. Creating moments of quiet time allows you to appreciate what becomes an inner peacefulness. It allows you to calm your mind, focus your attention, relax your body, and simply be in the present moment. You begin to appreciate how wonderful it is to stop doing and simply be when you remove yourself from the external world even for ten minutes every day, and focus on the world within.

In line with carving out alone time to simply be quiet with your thoughts (as well as creating moments of pure quiet), there are fundamental principles that need to be practiced and experienced in order to create a greater sense of self. These principles are simple yet priceless. If you can master them—ideally early on in your life—your capacity for self-knowledge and personal growth will become a driving force in how you live the rest of your life.

Governing Principles for Developing Your Sense of Self

1) Live on your own.

It may seem like a simple thing, but having the opportunity to live independent of your family of origin, to know what it means to be truly self-sufficient, to rely on you to take care of yourself and to make yourself happy, allows you to know completely and confidently that you can be independent and be okay. Living on your own (either alone, or with roommates) teaches you far more than any book or family member could possibly teach you about being autonomous and self-reliant. While the challenges of living independently are different from those of living with someone in a relationship, being on your own requires that you depend on your self first.

As much as you may have set cultural and ethnic customs that stipulate when you can appropriately move out on your own, living independent of your family teaches you the importance of relying on yourself for receiving what you need.

It is in those moments of feeling lonely and having to go within (into who you are) for comfort and self-reassurance, that you learn how to create happy. This reinforces the fact that you can be alone and be content. You may feel lonely from time to time, but you can survive apart from others. To be able to live on your own—to experience autonomy as your own self and be happy—is a major achievement.

2) Spend time alone each day in quiet reflection or in an activity that requires solitude.

I'm sure that some of us come by this more easily than others. It actually requires skill and discipline to intentionally carve out "alone time" away from other people.

(Being alone with your pets or in nature still counts as "alone time.")

Creating moments of quiet in order to reflect is crucial for connecting with your inner self and to get grounded. Being alone with your thoughts makes it easy to daydream, envisioning what you would like for your future.

To spend time each day alone in formal mediation, prayer, introspection, or guided visualization as well as having time each day to pursue quiet activities in solitude (even for short periods of time), ensures that you nurture your inner self. Create moments of quiet reflection and introspection in order to evaluate past behaviors as well as present-moment thoughts and feelings.

If being alone is difficult for you, explore why. Do you need to always be in the presence of others? In addition to your busy life, do you find yourself talking, socializing, emailing, and text messaging as a way of "staying connected" at all times? How would you describe your experience being alone with yourself? Can you be alone and be happy?

If being alone is a challenge, begin with easy steps. Plan an activity that you would normally seek the company of others to do, and go alone. For example, go to your fitness class alone rather than with a friend, skip lunch with your work colleagues and find a place where you can eat on your own (without checking emails on your Black-Berry). Have coffee in a café and watch the world go by outside rather than making it a social outing with friends. Make an effort to be alone at times throughout the day and take advantage of opportunities to be quiet with your thoughts (e.g. commuting without an iPod or car stereo, eating your lunch without a book or newspaper in front of you, lying in bed at night simply reflecting on the day, before falling asleep).

In no time, it does become easier, and more comfortable, to enjoy moments of solitude.

3) Figure out who you are.

Know what you stand for and what you believe in. At the same time, be open to new experiences and learning from others so that you continue to evolve.

The longer you exist on this planet, the more opportunity you have for figuring out who you are. Even as you spend much of your adolescence, and certainly your twenties, in self-discovery, you need to continue honoring the process of self-evolution by actively seeking out knowledge about yourself, and what is right for you. Knowing who you are—including your beliefs about others and the world—provides you with self-assurance. To never stop learning is to become more knowledgeable and to understand what you did not previously know.

You can certainly honor others' opinions and perspectives, but make it your responsibility to consider what you truly believe to be right for you. Remain open-minded as you hear new information and ideas so that you remain open to change your point of view as you learn. Be comfortable standing behind your word without needing to criticize another or be right. You continue to evolve by always building on your existing knowledge of yourself, and choosing to become more.

4) Breathe ... Meditate

It's what you already do as a function of life—now use your breath to clear your mind from all of the noise and clutter that exists in your head. Use your breathing to become quiet and to focus inwardly. Meditation is only a step away.

You can do informal meditation in as little as four or five minutes. This practice allows you to develop the skill of focused attention on your breath as you allow your mind to quiet. As you sit comfortably, simply observe your inhalation and exhalation. Remain open to whatever ideas or images come into your mind. Alternatively, you may choose a topic or ask a question of your higher consciousness and notice what information comes from that.

The practice of meditation is also helpful as you explore a particular idea or future goal. For example, breathe as you visualize a positive outcome that you would like to see (e.g. finding a life partner, or nurturing aspects of your existing love relationship).

As you develop a guided meditation practice (e.g. in the morning before you begin your day, at night before sleep), you train your unconscious mind to seek out what you really want. Like the mental rehearsal that elite athletes use as part of their high performance training, you shape your destiny by what you think about most.

5) Keep a journal.

Contrary to what preconceived ideas you may have (i.e. "I don't have time to journal," "What am I supposed to write about?" and "I don't like writing"), journaling is an immediate and spontaneous way of releasing the thoughts and feelings that you (often indefinitely) ruminate on. Expressing yourself through the written word provides an experience of catharsis as well as a formal process to observe and develop insights around what typically escapes you as fleeting thoughts.

As another way of focusing your attention inward, the process of journaling creates a steady stream of conscious thought. Writing requires extra time for your brain to process the words as opposed to your just thinking them. The brain now has a finite point at which to examine a particular thought, separate and complete from all of the others that enter your mind. The process of journaling is, in and of itself, largely therapeutic as a tool for learning and introspection.

Keeping a journal is a wonderful way to compile an ongoing list of the steps you have taken (including the challenges you have overcome) towards building a greater sense of self. Use your journal as a place to list all of the positive attributes you aspire to develop as well as those that you currently have. Journaling is a valuable way to affirm your developing sense of self.

6) Make *you* a priority every day.

Carving out time to do something that you enjoy reminds you that you need to do something every day to give back to your self. This can be as simple as going to the gym, reading a chapter or two of a novel you enjoy at bedtime, enjoying the outdoors as you walk through the park during your lunch break, or making the time to get a long-overdue haircut. These activities are what you choose to do purely for yourself. Making a priority to include these activities has a cumulative effect in nurturing your soul.

My client Sophie was desperately trying to change careers. She had developed a strategy of starting each workday by reviewing a short list of what she needed to do for herself. Because her job was so hectic, Sophie realized that if she didn't honor her commitment to "self" by taking care of simple daily life-tasks for herself, she would never be ready to leave her job. Making herself a priority meant that Sophie took daily small steps towards her life long goal of being a personal trainer. Each time she accomplished something on her list, Sophie was a step closer to living her dream.

Making you a priority involves conscious thought. It easily becomes habit and routine as you notice the benefits to your emotional well-being and psyche. Enhance your experience by being present and focusing all of your attention on what you are doing in that moment. Being present also heightens the quality of your experience, making it more memorable. (For example, you can exercise with intention to the specific muscle groups that you are working, giving your full attention and effort to that activity in each moment. To go to the gym and socialize with others or allow your thoughts to wander as you are exercising compromises your ability to concentrate on the task you are doing.)

Included in this category is the importance of building self-esteem. If you are a priority each day, you challenge yourself to appreciate all that you might take for granted. (e.g. your ability to speak three languages, your talent for remembering facts and details, your ability to solve problems and find the best solutions, and so on). You also look for ways in which you can challenge yourself to grow outside of your comfort zone as you acknowledge that to do so inspires you with confidence.

7) Consciously "work" on aspects of your self that need improving.

It's not enough to gain knowledge from your journaling, meditation, and quiet introspection. To develop your sense of self, you also need to be working actively on who it is that you desire to become. Evaluate the person that you are presently. Decide which qualities no longer serve you. Decide which qualities you still want to develop.

Enjoy the process of letting go of the old you and learning how to be the "new improved you." As you work on improving your self, enjoy and appreciate the "success moments" that you experience along the way.

Know that some changes will take longer because of your previous history of being a different way. In building self-efficacy, it's important that you actively work on making changes to yourself, so that you can begin to see even small results and feel encouraged to continue. As you see progress, you'll feel a sense of empowerment helping you maintain the momentum of change as you continue to seek out further challenges for personal growth.

Putting you first means that you have made the effort to know yourself. As you feel more comfortable in who you are it becomes easier to decide what is best and right for you at all times, to value yourself enough to decide the direction of your life perpetuates inner happiness.

If you can make yourself happy you don't need to rely on others to create happiness for you, rather they complement your quality of life and the happiness you experience in your life. Knowing that you can be happy independent of a love relationship gives you the freedom to decide who you choose to share yourself with and also when you no longer need to be in a relationship with a particular person.

To know yourself and to place the highest level of value on your life means that you make it a priority to live your life in a way that honors your self-worth. As you continue to develop your sense of self, you innately begin to search for the greater meaning of your existence.

Your Life's Purpose

Your life's purpose is your destiny. It is what you consciously choose to do with your life, using your unique gifts. These gifts are the inherent, innate, and also learned qualities that are specific to you. You fulfill your destiny by using your gifts to contribute in a meaningful way towards a greater good. In sharing of yourself and your gifts with others, you fulfill your life's purpose.

Using your innate gifts enables you to help others. Different from a good deed or "a random act of kindness," your life's purpose is a discernible talent that you become more skilled at as you continue to utilize it.

To know yourself is to identify your inherent talents and abilities. Your talents may include something as simple as being able to make others laugh, or to effectively bring people together for a common good. Your inherent ability to fix "things," to think creatively (and outside the box), or your love of dance and music are all aspects that uniquely shape your destiny and the direction of your life.

As your search for self continues, you uncover and explore many more of your inherent gifts. Healthy self-esteem and self-confidence perpetuates your ability to use and share your gifts. Defining your specific life's purpose becomes a natural extension of your desire to create a more fulfilling existence.

To help you define your life's purpose, answer the following questions with as much detail and information as possible:

- What do you most enjoy doing?
- What gives you inner fulfillment and purpose?
- What are you inherently good at?
- What abilities or skills come easily and naturally to you?
- How would you spend your day if you never again had to earn money?
- What do people come to you for help with?
- What are some activities you enjoyed as a child but per haps no longer do?

The above questions will hopefully inspire thoughts and ideas, which on some level you already knew to be true. In identifying and acknowledge your innate gifts, you can then create your life's purpose statement. Your life's purpose statement describes (usually in a sentence or two) what you envision and believe your specific purpose to be.

With your answers written in front of you, key words and phrases as well as emerging themes will help you formulate a statement inclusive of what you believe to be your particular gifts or talents. Think about how you can use these innate abilities to help others in some way. This begins the creation of your life's purpose statement.

Acknowledge the perfect connection that exists between using your gifts and fulfilling your life's purpose. Using your free will to make choices that are in line with what makes you happiest moves you in the direction of your life's purpose. As you realize your unique purpose in this world, you begin to live your destiny.

In a love relationship your life's purpose needs to be supported.

Couples who co-exist in the absence of identifying their particular purpose continue to search (even on an unconscious level) for the greater meaning for their lives. Establishing a particular purpose for your life allows you to feel personally fulfilled beyond being in relationship. In your quest for defining and living your purpose, your love relationship becomes an important adjunct to the meaning you experience in your life, rather than the center of your existence.

When you build your life around your partner, children, or extended family you can't help but ignore vital aspects of your self. Similarly, when you choose an occupation or profession that you find neither enjoyable nor meaningful, you are left feeling empty and without purpose. In denying or ignoring what has heartfelt importance—what inspires you to be more—you cannot ever feel completely fulfilled or satisfied. The desire to spend the majority of your waking moments participating in activities that contribute to your sense of happiness is the best motivator (at any age) to identify and live your life's purpose.

Chapter Four

Practice Makes Perfect:
The REAL Purpose of Dating

You become accomplished at love when you have opportunities to practice and to apply what you have learned from each experience.

The archetypal definition of true monogamy is virtually unattainable in Western civilization, although having only one partner throughout an entire lifetime continues to be possible in those societies that encourage pre-pubescent, arranged marriages. With the rare exception of "high-school sweethearts"—cases where a young couple exclusively dates and then marries—true monogamy is an extinct concept. In fact, the social mores and customs of our modern culture encourage an extensive (and perhaps an even more casual) variety of relationship experiences. Alas dating, as we know it, is an essential element in our quest for a mate.

In the same way that it takes repeated effort and discipline to develop mastery of a skill (e.g. playing sport at a competitive level, excelling in your profession, or mastering a new language), you have an opportunity—initially during adolescence and then adulthood—to "practice" (and ultimately become successful) at being in a love relationship. If you can remain consciously aware and attentive throughout what typically ends up being a solid decade or more of pivotal dating experiences, then you will cumulatively learn more about yourself and others then you could ever imagine.

With each significant love relationship comes a possibility for moving closer to your ideal. If you continue to choose people who embrace the qualities and attributes that are vitally important to you (e.g. strength of character, honesty, sense of humor, high morals, and so on), as well as apply what you have learned from previous relationships (including those you observed within your family of origin), you ultimately move closer to finding what so many refer to as a soul mate or "great love." This ideal is someone with whom you can completely be yourself and with whom you mutually grow and evolve.

How might you be different if you were taught to value your love relationships as inherent opportunities for self-growth? What if you viewed dating as a fundamental element in your discovery of self and as practice towards how you want your ideal love relationship to be? Rather than as a means to an end, could you embrace dating as an affirmative ritual of self-growth and self-actualization?

As you reflect back over your experiences of dating, what have you learned? What was it about who you were at the time that allowed you to succeed at being in a relationship however short-lived it may have been? Conversely, what was it about who you were that made your relationship less successful? Just as your previous experiences serve as important ways to learn about what you most want in an ideal future love relationship, they also highlight your flaws and insecurities, forcing you to work on those qualities within yourself that you acknowledge need changing. The experiences of dating offer important opportunities to learn how to be in relationship, and "in love" while at the same time, learning a great deal about yourself.

In my practice, I see clients who have recently come out of— or are in the process of disengaging from—unhealthy relationships. Even if they can remotely conceive of dating again at some future time in their lives, the idea is both daunting and discouraging. The common perception of dating is that it is the unpleasant and uncomfortable process that people they have to go through if they ultimately want to find true love.

Perhaps you married your "first love"and, as a result, have had limited practice dating. Perhaps you have had a few relationships, none of which would be considered serious, before marrying early in life and soon thereafter starting a family. Or perhaps you married a partner because of circumstance (e.g. expecting a child, emigrating to another country, or as an arranged marriage). Whatever the situation, the common element is the notion of having limited experiences and opportunities to meet and get to know new people. In a word ... to "date."

The experience of dating is paramount to what becomes the quintessential preparation for establishing a healthy love relationship. The experience that you gain from dating means that you can then make the best possible, informed decision for your future.

Dating: Essential Guidelines

1) Know what you want—the ideal mate list.

Create a list of qualities that you want in a mate. Make your list as inclusive and detailed as possible; nothing is too small to overlook. Items of particular importance to you may include:

- openness and honesty: someone who can easily share their thoughts and feelings
- respectful towards you and others
- trustworthy
- kind
- generous
- helpful and considerate
- thoughtful: e.g. will ask if you need anything if they are going to the supermarket
- loving: e.g. spontaneously affectionate
- embraces new experiences and adventures
- positive and optimistic
- acts with integrity

- enjoys spending time with your family and loves your family members as their own
- is supportive of your career and life goals
- shares equally in household responsibilities
- a non-smoker
- is healthy and physically active
- doesn't snore
- appreciates nature and the outdoors
- loves animals

After you consider some of the more general character traits, include the smaller items, ones that you may overlook because you just assume that these will be part of the ideal person. Remember that it's important to create a comprehensive list. You can always choose to prioritize the most crucial (what I refer to as "deal breaker") items later.

Your list needs to be well thought out so that you will be reminded of all of the things that are most important to you once you begin to compare potential "candidates."

Many people tend to overlook priority items on their unwritten list and rationalize behaviors in order to make possible candidates "fit." I'm suggesting an actual, written list so you can refer to it as you date, and as you enter into a committed relationship. Once you have your list, you can make reference to the top priority items, the absence of which would be "deal breakers"—in other words, the most important things that you can't live without. These top priority items are usually ones that you are able to assess quickly, either visually or through a brief conversation, making it easy for you to focus on those people who embrace what is most important to you. Some of your top five (or ten!) deal breakers may include such characteristics as: a positive attitude, loves children and animals, can easily communicate their feelings, trustworthy, honest, and has high integrity.

The objective of consciously choosing the best possible mate is to have a life partner who has all of the *most critical* traits and qualities that are important to you and most of the others. Without a list of ideal qualities, you are less likely to remain loyal to what you truly want, and more inclined to overlook the red flags, focusing on the qualities that you find appealing rather than paying close attention to the ones that are missing. As you continue to be in relationship with that particular person, you have a bigger and bigger investment in overlooking problems and issues for the sake of validating your decision to remain in that relationship.

When I first sat down with Lisa she could not find anything positive to say about her four-year relationship with Russell. The two had been living together (with Lisa's son Zackary) for the past two years. Lisa addressed countless issues in therapy, but for each one she had a convincing example or "reason" why she had continued in the relationship. Since Russell had always been jealous of the attention and love Lisa freely gave to Zackary, he would pick on Zackary for just about everything including the way in which he did his chores, and for being too dependent on Lisa. Recently, Lisa reported, Russell had begun hiding Zackary's favorite foods. (She found a jar of peanut butter at the bottom of the laundry hamper.) Among the many problems in their relationship, Lisa couldn't overlook Russell's behavior toward her son.

One of the reasons why Lisa had been able to continue in the relationship was that she was an eternal optimist. When she confronted Russell with a problem, he would typically apologize and promise to change. Lisa wanted so badly to believe that things could get better that she convinced herself that they would. Lisa rationalized her intuitive voice in order to create agreement between what Russell promised and what she ideally wanted. The problem was that Lisa was quickly losing patience waiting for Russell to change.

In the course of a few sessions, Lisa began to examine her love relationship from a place of consciousness. She began to recognize the difference between being patient and denying what she knew was inevitable. One of the things that helped solidify her decision to finally end the relationship was creating her ideal mate list. As Lisa read the many qualities and characteristics that she truly desired, she realized that she had stayed in this relationship far too long. Being consciously aware rather than "living in a fog" as she had described, meant that she could no longer pretend that things would be okay.

For Lisa, her truth was tied up in making the responsible decision for both herself and Zackary. As she moved in the direction that she knew was right, it felt easier. Within a couple of months of acting on her truth, Lisa had her house listed on the market, had found an apartment for her and Zackary, and was pleasantly surprised to see that Russell finally took her seriously. This time he didn't plead and beg her to stay.

For those of you who have resumed (or are contemplating) dating at some point after the end of a long-term committed relationship, referring to your "ideal mate" list will encourage you to stay focused on what you want. It often paints a clear picture of someone very different from the person that you were previously in relationship with.

Having a written list of all of the ideal traits you want in a mate allows you to feel hopeful (and excited) by the possibility that you know exactly (perhaps for the first time in your life) what you are looking for. It also provides you with a guaranteed method of "short-listing" all of the potential candidates that you meet.

In the end, your eventual life mate may have a quick temper, be somewhat forgetful, and need nine hours of sleep every night to your six, however, your list will provide you with a tool to appropriately discern what you can live with and what you can't.

You can end up with a partner who has all of the most important qualities that you are looking for. If your partner is doing the same thing, you can be sure that they will have similar qualities checked off on a list when choosing you!

2) Ask all of the important questions—*all* of them!

Asking the "right" questions means asking the questions that you need to have answered. This implies that you already know what it is that you are looking for in an ideal mate and from your love relationship. Don't worry that you sound like you are conducting a full-scale interview—because you are. As you ask the appropriate questions, listen carefully to what you hear. While you might want to think the best of someone, or even hope that their response on a particular issue might change with time, you need to remain extremely honest with yourself about what you're hearing.

Next, give yourself permission to probe! Refrain from deciding that you know what someone means when they answer your question. Your job is to find out exactly what their thoughts are (since there are always going to be things left unsaid in a conversation) rather than to assume that you already know the answer. It is your responsibility to follow up, clarify, and understand the answer so that there can be no confusion later. For example, "I haven't really thought about having kids" doesn't mean that it's an open possibility. The same response could also mean "I haven't really thought about having kids because I am quite content in my life without them."

Hearing answers that are not in line with what you are looking for are potential "red flags." Red flag items can be deal breakers. They are major differences in beliefs, lifestyles, dreams, or goals that can ultimately end a relationship or leave you feeling miserable as you continue in it. Acknowledging a red flag when it is presented and paying attention to it is extremely important. Couples who reach an impasse on a particular issue at some point further into their relationship are often discussing the same issue that they originally had opposing views on. Rarely do our belief systems change unless we choose to change them, so it's wise to know the potential issues from the beginning. You can then decide if that difference is something that you can live with.

Too often, I hear divorced couples speak about the red flags that they initially saw or heard in the early stages of their relationship, but chose to overlook or deny. Remember, red flag issues always catch up with you. It doesn't mean that a couple can't move past them, but to do so usually means that one person needs to make a 180-degree change of mind on that particular issue. It's far better to acknowledge major points of difference at the beginning of your love relationship and even to discuss how you will potentially deal with them when they surface, as this can save you a lot of time and heartache.

Being honest and upfront with your partner about a potential red flag, even though it might seem easier to look the other way, means that you can begin discussing a strategy for solving it. If the red flag issue is critically important to both people, and if your difference continues to remain irresolvable, then the relationship is likely destined to end.

3) "Eyes wide open"

As much as each of us would like to believe that we accept others for who they are, we often impose our personal ideas and opinions on those closest to us, in the hopes that we might convince them otherwise. In other words, we look for others to make changes based on what we would like to see. Sadly, our efforts become hopelessly lost as we begin to realize that nothing can change another person except their own willingness to change. Sometimes you can have a positive influence on the changes your partner decides to make, but to expect that you will be able to "cure" your mate of all of their bad habits means you risk fighting a losing battle—and it usually does end up being a battle!

If you can see your partner for all of their wonderful attributes as well as their flaws then you have the workings of an honest relationship. True love is not blind. True love is seeing your mate exactly as they are and loving them inclusive of their flaws. If your mate has the majority of the qualities that you've identified as ideal, you can feel assured that all of these positive characteristics will be more than enough to carry you through the rough spots in your relationship and more than enough to remind you of how fortunate you are.

Accept your partner for who they are, in this moment. See them with your eyes wide open.

4) Be strong enough to walk away.

After taking the time to figure out what you want, remain true to yourself. Know what you can accept in a life mate and what you cannot. Be confident in your ability to find what you want without accepting less than that. (If you still feel doubtful or hopeless about your ability to find what you are looking for, this illuminates your need to further develop your own sense of self.) Walking away from a relationship that doesn't contribute to your life in a positive way means that you have now created the possibility of having the kind of relationship that you really want. Don't settle for anything less.

If you are currently in a love relationship, pay attention to what is working and what is not working. I can vividly remember looking at a calendar my friend had posted above her desk at work. There were a combination of check marks ✔ and Xs placed on each of the days that had passed. As I quickly glanced at the entire month, I saw a majority of Xs, and only a handful or so of ✔. When I asked about the coded calendar, my friend described her method of "tracking" the state of her relationship. The Xs, as you can imagine, were strategically placed where she wanted to identify days (or in some cases a period of time, i.e. morning or afternoon) when there was conflict or turmoil in her relationship. This is the most explicit example of tracking relationship "behavior" that I have ever come across.

It would be months before this particular relationship reached a violent and destructive climax, one that could probably have been prevented if my friend had acted on the information that her calendar provided. Sometimes even the most obvious methods of observation can't help us if we aren't prepared to see what it shows us.

Many people will try their best to hold an unhealthy relationship together, even when they know it's not working, because they are afraid of (or don't enjoy) being alone. Society still places a high value on couples who are able to remain married for multiple decades. Being married and being happy are not necessarily mutually inclusive. Believing that the person you really want is out there can take away some of the fear.

Finding the Best ... Song?

It is when you can be completely honest with yourself that you begin to know whether your current love relationship is the best one for you. All couples experience periods in their life where they find themselves struggling to feel good about their love relationship—even questioning whether they have made the right choice. When you acknowledge the quiet voice inside you come to know what is best, even if you can't always act on it. When clients describe feeling confused about whether to remain in or leave their present relationship, I often use the following analogy. I remind them that making decisions in dating can be a bit like choosing which song to listen to on their car stereo.

Think of searching through the various pre-selected radio stations while driving your car. Do you immediately stop and listen once you find a song that you like, or do you continue searching through the remaining stations until you have previewed them all, and then come back to the best one based on how you feel at that moment?

While there is no right or wrong answer to this question, many people admit that they typically stop searching and simply listen once they find a song that they like. Most would admit that they would rather be enjoying music than spending time searching through all of their pre-programmed stations.

This analogy works to describe what most people tend to do when selecting a potential partner as well. Rather than hold out for what we ultimately want in a love relationship, are we too quick to pick from a limited selection? How can we possibly know what the best song is if we haven't heard what's playing on all of the stations?

How can you pick the best person to spend your life with if you choose from a limited number and without knowing exactly what you are looking for?

Dating ensures that you have an opportunity to find that best person. Assuming that you have done your homework and have a good sense of what you want in a life partner, dating is the mechanism that allows you to find that special someone. The clearer you are about what you want and don't want, the closer you can come to finding that.

What is rarely discussed about dating is the way it can act as a series of stepping-stones. With each new love relationship, you have the opportunity to come closer to finding your ideal. What I continue to see all around me are great examples of people who have stopped short of finding their ideal. They have gone with the good song on preset button two without checking the remaining 10 preset buttons, but had they checked, they would have found their favorite song playing on a station programmed on preset button eight. But they decided to settle for what was playing on two. Yes, I said it—settle!

Settling (for many reasons) continues to happen in real life.

If you pay close attention, each love relationship can bring you closer to your ideal, provided that you continue to hold out for what you most want. Each relationship has the possibility of being better than the one just before it.

By identifying the best qualities from your previous relationships, you can ensure that your next relationship will have more of what is most important to you. Each relationship has the ability to act as a stepping-stone, offering more of what you want in an ideal mate until you end up with at least 92% of what you are looking for.

Holding Out for 92%

When communication in a love relationship begins to break down or when external life situations present new or ongoing challenges for one or both members of a couple, it is the degree of compatibility and the congruency of values and beliefs that ultimately provides the basis for resilience. This is where the 92% becomes significantly important.

If you have a great deal in common with your partner (including the ideal qualities that you both believe are crucial), then it will be far easier navigating through the rough spots. Every person in a relationship experiences times (even fleeting moments) when they contemplate life without the other person. Knowing that you have chosen the best possible person to share your life with helps immensely. In fact, it's the 92%, the solid foundation that is built on compatibility factors including similar values and beliefs, that ensures that there is a significant foundation to support and sustain your love relationship, as each of you are busy struggling with inevitable day-to-day issues and life dilemmas.

If you think back to your previous love relationships, what was the underlying reason for their eventual ending? In most cases, even when you didn't initiate "termination," the relationships ended because of a lack of fundamental compatibility. The compatibility factor (whether you consciously recognize this or not) is also the reason why you know whether you would be interested in seeing someone for a second date. The more that you initially establish you have in common, the more likely it is that you will want to know more about a new person.

Having a list of ideal qualities and traits means that you have a simple yet very effective tool for knowing precisely the kind of mate that you want. An ideal list means that you have spent time thinking about what is most important in a life partner. Having made a thorough list, you don't need to take it along on every date. Rather, having gone through the exercise of creating such a list makes it far easier for you to simply know exactly what it is that you want, and to look for it.

Expecting that you will find at least 80% or 85% of what you are looking for in a life partner means that you will continue to search until you find it. (The exact same phenomenon occurs when you limit yourself.) If you believe that you "won't find someone better," then you conveniently stop looking, and you do everything possible to hold onto Mr. or Ms. "pretty good"—or worse Mr. or Ms. "wrong." Unfortunately, I repeatedly see examples of couples that have settled for what they think is "good enough" or "good on paper." Just settling when choosing a mate will not prove to be enough to sustain you in the difficult times, to endure the many distractions and challenges that inevitably occur as part of life, or (and perhaps most important) to nourish the changing desires and needs of both members of the couple as they change over time.

Having 92% compatibility means that your love relationship is founded on the values, beliefs, and goals that are most important to you both. Obviously, you can only determine this if both partners are fully honest and up-front with each other. If you conveniently go along with what your partner says or does for fear of creating conflict, you are not being true to your self or honoring who you are in the relationship.

If both of you are doing this, the problem is made even worse. You both receive incorrect information, which in turn, you both make further decisions on. It becomes a spiral of self (and other) deception if you can't be who you really are (even if that means acknowledging moments when you don't have a particular opinion or "don't know" how you feel).

Having 92% compatibility is also important since you don't remain the same person. Whether you resist change or not, you undoubtedly evolve (even ever so slightly) with time. Since some (or much) of what you initially believed in may change over the course of your love relationship, it needs to have enough (92% or more, in fact) of a solid foundation that it can support and withstand the changes in who you and your partner continue to become. When all of the fundamental basics are there from the beginning it becomes far easier to love and to continue desiring the relationship as time goes on.

Love relationships that embody 92% compatibility ensure a deeply rooted sense of stability and commitment to one another, allowing each member of the couple to embrace new challenges and to seek out opportunities for change and the awareness of raising self-esteem as a means of self-actualization or realizing their full potential. Couples who recognize the value of working on their individual self-esteem can easily see evidence of how it benefits their love relationship.

Conscious Choice

Consistent in the literature on couple relationships is the suggestion that we unconsciously choose mates who possess both the positive and negative traits of our parents in our family of origin. An example of how our unconscious choices affect our mate selection comes from my work with Bernadette. Devon's greatest initial attraction for Bernadette was now the very thing that she most resented. Devon's drive and ambition were initially very appealing since, as she explained, her own parents seemed to have little drive to make a better life for their family.

Devon's ability to be emotionally available (to be there for her when she needed to talk, to encourage her and offer suggestions and help, as well as care for her physical, emotional, and financial needs) was an endearing quality since in Bernadette's own family of origin both parents were largely distant and unresponsive. In fact, Bernadette's mother left the family home when Bernadette was young, leaving her to care for herself and her younger siblings.

In many ways, this left Bernadette without the capacity to be emotionally available for anyone. Overwhelmed with emotional and physical responsibilities at a very young age, Bernadette never had the experience of having her own emotional needs met. Her father, who was able to provide for the family in monetary ways (as does Devon now), could not provide Bernadette with unconditional love and support. As a result, Bernadette grew up with low self-esteem and a poor self-image.

Because our rationale for choosing a mate occurs predominantly on an unconscious level, it is quite common to find yourself knee-deep in familiar patterns of being, long before you become aware of what is happening. Not only do you choose partners with similar attributes (both positive and negative) to your parents but you also tend to repeat familiar and well-established behavioral patterns based on your "learned model" for how to be in relationship.

In recognizing your well-established patterns, you can begin to understand how you need to be different in order to have the kind of love relationship you actually want. You can then choose a partner with full consciousness, and based on a well-informed model for what a healthy love relationship looks like.

In many cases it's not until your love relationship comes to an end, that you begin to reflect on your experiences and behaviors while in that relationship. Examining your well-established ways of being is necessary if you want to be able to consciously choose how you react and behave in any of your future relationships. Without consciousness, you are likely to look for the same traits in a partner, and to repeat what you have always done.

To learn from your love relationships, you must be present and self-aware. You must consciously choose your destiny while in your love relationship in order to live your life on purpose.

Choosing Consciously

Take a closer, more conscious, look at your current love relationship by answering the following questions honestly, with as much detail as possible:

1. What characteristics or personality traits do you find most appealing / least appealing about your mate?

_____
_____
_____

2. Which of these characteristics are similar to one or both of your parents?

_____
_____
_____

3. How have you personally grown or evolved as a result of being in this relationship?

_____
_____
_____

4. What lessons do you still need to learn in order to be the person you want to be?

_____
_____
_____

5. What traits do you possess that allow you to help your mate evolve and grow?

_____
_____
_____

6. What traits does you mate possess that allow you to evolve and grow?

_____

_____

_____

7. How will you continue to be challenged to grow by remaining in this love relationship?

_____

_____

_____

Answering these questions in your journal will provide a way for you to reflect on the reasons you chose your partner as well as the greater purpose for your being in relationship together. It is also important to think about what life lessons you may still need to learn in being together.

Choosing wisely is perhaps the most substantial prerequisite for creating a fulfilling love relationship. While it is an incredible feeling to revel in the excitement of spending time with someone who seems perfectly wonderful, there is purpose to having your eyes wide open, seeing everything exactly as it is. Getting to know someone extremely well means that you are always honest and truthful about what you see. The potential for an authentic and honest relationship is greatest when you remain aware of all of the qualities of your potential mate when making the decision about how well-suited or compatible you are. Of course, remember this presupposes that you know exactly what you want in a life partner.

Each of us has the ability to see with absolute clarity, and if you rationalize the problem aspects of your relationship in the hope that these will either change or go away (neither of which ever happens) you are quite deliberately deceiving yourself. You become hopeful that somehow everything will take care of itself. Yet, your gut knows better. Ignoring the "red flags" (e.g. a lack of passion or sexual chemistry, differences between you in core attributes or values, or reoccurring and potentially irresolvable issues that continue to surface) is about the worst thing that you can do at the beginning of any new relationship. Those same issues will continue to surface and actually end up becoming bigger and more problematic unless they are addressed and resolved.

To address and resolve a "red flag" issue, both members of a couple must participate in open and honest dialogue about the problem, and then effectively change certain behaviors and ways of being.

Without conscious awareness, you end up choosing a partner similar to what you have always known. Without conscious awareness, you tend to behave, believe in, and react to events in the same way as you did in previous relationships. You end up believing that you have bad luck in love, when instead, what you are doing is choosing without consciousness. Because you haven't evolved, your choice in a mate hasn't either.

ɔ3

It would be several months after that pivotal, thought-provoking conversation until Ryan and I first decided to go out together socially. Neither of us actually thought of our first outing as an official date, since our well-established friendship made the outing platonically low-pressure.

I believe that the universe has a particularly blatant way of getting your attention when it needs to point out something of Consequential Importance. All you have to do is pay attention.

What started out as an informal evening became more and more extraordinary—and magical—as we shared intellectually stimulating conversation, jokes, laughter, and a surreal ease of communicating with one another. By the time Ryan dropped me off back at home, I knew that someone unbelievably incredible had just entered my life.

Chapter Five

Real Love

Real love does mean forever.

Real love is not blind. Real love means that you are able to see another human being as they are and love them inclusively.

While this book is about love relationships, love is a fundamental human experience. If you consider the concept of love as having no boundaries or limits, then it becomes necessary to define it as a global construct first, and then define how it is within a couple relationship.

Real or authentic love is unyielding and limitless in its capacity. Real love is given freely and completely. On a basic human level, love is actually one of the easiest and most pure emotions that we can experience. It is only because of our humanness—our intellectual capabilities and our ego—that we struggle with an incessant need to analyze, critique, and judge something as incredible and simple as love.

When you open yourself up to expressing love free of any limits or boundaries, it becomes far easier to behave in a loving way more of the time. Love as a human construct is not limited to familial or romantic relationships. On a fundamental level, to operate out of a place of love exists as easily as:

- taking time out of your life to listen to a co-worker express their excitement about buying their first home—and being genuinely happy for them;

- responding to a elderly stranger's request for help by providing them with directions, and then walking with them a half block out of your way to show them which bus to take to get to their destination; or

- taking cut flowers from your garden to a neighbor.

To be loving—to express love outwardly—takes many forms. Deliberate acts of love occur all around you each day. You may call them acts of kindness, but these actions are created out of a loving heart. You behave in a loving way out of intention—a conscious desire—to express kindness and compassion for another human being. Real love in its purest form has no limits. All acts of love are of consequence.

C03

The purpose of love is in its experience. It is in experiencing love that you feel compelled to be loving in your actions with others. The power of love is in its experience. As you act out of love (even with the smallest gesture), you create positive experiences for others. As you experience the positive gratification that comes from eliciting acts of love, your consciousness grows. You realize the ease to which you can initiate loving behaviors, and you become more inspired to do so. To love and to be loved gives you a purpose in this world in which to thrive.

If you are consciously aware, you may notice the experience of love originating in your heart region. It comes as little surprise as to how the heart has long been associated with love. As you continue to observe, the feeling is immediately expansive and courses through your entire body. Some refer to love as a "high," euphoria, and certainly the chemicals released in your brain (e.g. serotonin, vasopressin, and oxytocin) when you experience feelings of love, strongly support this. It is through experiencing real love that you are able to share it selflessly.

C03

If you asked most couples how they knew that they were in love, many would describe a concurrent experience of intense closeness and intimacy (with or without the physical act of sex), an emotional connection (achieved through mutual communication, and sharing of one's innermost thoughts and feelings), and attachment (a unrelenting desire to be with that particular person with some level of permanence). Some couples also describe a spiritual or soulful connection with their mate. (These types of relationships are discussed in detail in Chapter Eight).

It's easier to proclaim your love for someone during moments of intense joy, in the midst of romance or sexual intimacy, or generally as your relationship is going well. It's much more difficult to love a person without conditions.

Are you able to love your partner unconditionally during a heated argument, when you are angry with them? Can you love someone when you are no longer "in love" with them? Are there limits to real love?

As you are about to proclaim your love to someone for the first time, be aware of whether you love them based on that particular moment, their actions, who you perceive them to be, or how you feel when you are with them. Real love means that you continue to love a person even when you are no longer "in love" with them. Real love means that you go on loving someone even after your relationship has ended and your individual lives take you in different directions.

To experience real love toward another human being requires that you fundamentally like who they are. Love relationships based on mutual friendship, respect, and shared values and beliefs have greater resilience and compatibility. To be able to experience real love spontaneously, effortlessly, and with an endless capacity requires that you are able to experience it of your self.

Self-Love

Self-love honors all that you are. It is the basis for self-esteem and self-worth. It is not based in ego or placing self first at the expense of others. Self-love is an essential and elemental property in developing and maintaining a healthy sense of self. It is far easier to know your self honestly and completely when you like, and ideally love, the person that you are.

Without self-love, you lack the confidence of knowing that you are able to provide basic needs and desires for yourself. As successful as you may be (as a parent, in your role at work, as a sibling, friend, or mentor), without self-love you continue to struggle with feeling worthy and emotionally independent. You rely on others for evidence of your value and self-worth, and continue to question evidence even when it is presented to you.

Without self-love, your desire to love others (and to feel validated through loving and receiving love from others) often overrides your need to provide necessary self-love and self-care behaviors. Without self-love you may believe that you are giving love infinitely and unselfishly. Yet, upon closer examination (and with self-honesty), it is likely that your demonstrations of love are related to self-validation and at times, driven out of fear (e.g. believing and behaving based on the inherent worry that if you don't give of yourself completely and fully, your loved one will lose interest and no longer love you).

Without self-love you are likely to continue in relationships that are no longer authentically contributing to your source of personal happiness. In fact, remaining in love relationships long after they have completed their purpose, limits (and begins to have a negative impact on) your personal well-being and growth.

Self-love behaviors facilitate incredible healing on an emotional, spiritual, and energetic level. While each of us has our own personal experiences of what constitutes unconditional love, we all have the capacity to learn how to love our self, and others, unconditionally.

Examples of Healthy "Self-Love" Behaviors

• Pay attention to what you need in any given moment and respond to those needs accordingly. Take action to learn what your needs are by practicing self-awareness.

- Speak up ("using your voice") to express your needs. Honor what you believe to be right and best for you even though it may be different from that of your mate (or others).

- Make time each day to do things that nurture your soul (e.g. take a walk at lunch so that you can enjoy the outdoors as you create some time all to yourself, go to the gym, listen to the kind of music that you most enjoy, rebuild the engine in your muscle car, enjoy a long, hot bath, get a massage, and so on).

- Take care of your self first, by attending to your fundamental needs (e.g. self-care, exercise, proper sleep, healthy eating).

- Say "no" (without guilt or angst) as a way of honoring what is right for you. (Those that truly care about and respect you will honor your answer of "no.")

Self-love behaviors are modeled out of self-efficacy and the importance of honoring your needs. Self-love behaviors are instinctively practiced if you have healthy self-esteem.

Without self-love, you are less likely to take optimal care of your physical, emotional, and mental health. Being the "best Mom" for your four-year old daughter, but neglecting many of your basic needs (e.g. sleep, exercise, time alone, intimacy with your partner) in order to do so, indicates a need for greater self-love. Allowing yourself to be bullied by an aging parent even though you are an adult with your own grown family exemplifies low self-love. Remaining in a love relationship where your partner is verbally abusive and disrespectful would suggest dangerously unhealthy levels of self-love.

Having difficulty standing up for yourself, taking care of your self and your basic needs—which then allows you to be your best with others—or doing the simple activities that nurture you indicates self-love that needs attention and work.

In a love relationship, you experience how your capacity to love another increases exponentially the more self-love and self-respect you possess. (If you don't quite believe this, then take a close look around you. Pay attention to how someone in a relationship is treated when their partner lacks self-love and respect. Pay attention to the limitations, the expectations for reciprocation, and the value placed on "self" over another when self-love is absent). Condoning this same behavior also occurs when you lack the self-love to place appropriate and healthy boundaries around what is and is not acceptable.

Even if you are currently in a love relationship, it is crucial that you continue to work on aspects of yourself. Love relationships allow you to simultaneously work on and heal issues from your past (even if you are not always conscious of this benefit). Being able to give unconditional love to another being is much easier and requires far less effort when you know how to love your self. While your love relationship provides an intimate mechanism for you to learn, to grow, to gain self-confidence, and to heal, many people in relationship continue to neglect their own needs, including the basic human need for self-esteem.

If you deny or ignore your own needs, eventually this catches up with you. You are left feeling empty (as if something important is lacking) because you have abandoned your own needs in place of giving to your loved ones. One of the most incredible gifts of a love relationship is the reminder of your own value and self-worth so that you can continue to practice self-love while being in relationship.

When I first met Eliana, I was not quite sure how to read her. A tall and beautiful woman, Eliana looked intensely serious at first glance. And yet, when she spoke her voice was soft and gentle. As she began to talk, I could hear a resounding sadness within her. An immigrant from Russia, Eliana struggled with the values she was raised by, some of which she now wholeheartedly rejected, and those of the country she had immigrated to.

Eliana's biggest dilemma was love. She had recently separated from her husband and had sole custody of their six-year-old son.

Eliana had left Damian not because she didn't love him but because she loved him at the expense of her own self.

Eliana believed that love was enough. Her self-proclaimed obsession for Damian meant that Eliana overlooked what was missing or wrong and instead focused on being everything to him. The problem was that Eliana loved Damian to the exclusion of herself.

Over time, she began to realize that Damian was not able to love selflessly in return. In withholding love from her, Damian used manipulation (knowing that Eliana would do anything for him), to get what he wanted. Eliana's resilient willingness to receive conditional love from Damian made her emotionally dependent and thus vulnerable.

Even after leaving her seven-year marriage, Eliana couldn't stop loving Damian.

Living on her own, Eliana felt imprisoned by her emotions. While Damian was quite content to see her occasionally and have romantic dates, Eliana remained hopeful that he would change, and continued to hope that Damian could develop the capacity for giving her unconditional love. In the meantime, with Damian showing no signs of this, Eliana felt "broken."

When you give unconditional love in a healthy relationship, you do so as you give unconditional love to yourself first. If you consistently put your partner's wants and desires in front of your own, you end up sacrificing your needs, and slowly losing your sense of self. Love relationships cannot be sustained when one partner continually gives all of their self to the exclusion of their own happiness and worth. Self-sacrifice is not a property of a healthy love relationship. It undermines the notion of self-preservation and the ability to experience nurturing and self-love first and foremost.

In practicing unconditional self-love, you gain the knowledge of what it means to be capable of accepting and receiving love as an experience. You learn how important self-love is to feeling whole and complete. To provide yourself with a mechanism for accepting and receiving love means that you honor your place in this world and the value that you offer.

Unconditional love is healing as it allows you to accept the person that you are even as you may continue to seek more. As you work on evolving and improving your self, unconditional love offers acceptance and trust that your efforts toward this are significantly important. You become more and you believe in your ability to deserve more as you experience first-hand what it feels like to honor your self.

CB

To love another human being is first to be wholly committed to the process of loving your self even more. Affirming your self-love means that you rely on yourself completely as the source of your own personal happiness. To say that someone else "makes" you happy because of who they are, what they did, said, or gave (or bought for) you defies your ability to provide yourself with what you really need.

One of the inherent problems we face is our inability to provide love for our self. We believe that in loving someone, our needs will be taken care of and we will be loved. This is not so. In order to experience authentic happiness you need to provide unconditional love for yourself. To love yourself means that you can enjoy the experience love firsthand, and that you do not depend on others to love you.

You define your existence by knowing that you can provide for yourself what you need at any time. To exude self-love means that you are able to provide and experience love for yourself—independent of being loved by others.

What many of us do not formally learn is how to love ourselves so much, that we are kind and forgiving to the person we are. Most of us have not been formally taught that to love others unconditionally is easiest when we can love our self unconditionally first. Unconditional self-love is difficult when you are caught up in negative or self-effacing thoughts. Your inner thoughts are powerful in their directing force. If you place conditions on your self-love and self-acceptance (e.g. "If I can just lose 30 pounds then I will feel better (and I can finally love myself," or "If I land this job then I can feel successful (and I can fully love myself,") you rarely feel happy with who you are in this moment. You continue to search for what you think will make your self happy rather than be happy with who your self already is.

To love your self unconditionally requires that you are patient and accepting of yourself all of the time. You work towards this by practicing self-love behaviors daily. You strive to be conscious of your inner thoughts in moments when you are less than loving of yourself, in order to become more self-aware. Self-awareness gives you the freedom to make choices rather than operate as you have always done. To be self-aware means that you can choose to be loving and compassionate to yourself. Without the experience of self-love you have little capacity to fully experience and internalize, the love of others.

It's important to continue practicing unconditional self-love simply because it remains a fundamental element of self-acceptance and healing throughout life.

Unconditional Love

In a love relationship, your most important job is simply to give love unconditionally. Unconditional love is love given freely and fully from your highest self. It is love free of any and all attachments to material and personal gain. When you love unconditionally, there are no expectations in receiving.

In a spiritually conscious love relationship, both partners are easily able to give and receive unconditional love. Even though you may, at times, say hurtful things and be unkind, a spiritually conscious relationship is one in which you can easily acknowledge your human limitations, and willingly make every effort to behave differently.

In a healthy love relationship, the assumption is that you are not giving unconditional love as a way of "overlooking" or "ignoring" situations where you are repeatedly treated poorly or where your self-respect or personal safety is compromised.

When you love unconditionally, you refrain from judging your mate or others based on your standards, allowing them to instead live by the standards they have chosen. You accept your mate and their choices based on their self-development, at any given time.

If you can allow yourself to love others without conditions, to forgive and accept limitations or shortcomings, to simply love instead of being angry, and to be loving and kind without placing judgment or blame, then you can say that you have mastered the ability to love unconditionally. How easy it is to demonstrate unconditional love on a daily basis is ultimately dependant on your capacity for forgiveness and acceptance of others.

As a learned construct, your initial experiences of unconditional love typically occur during your formative years (from your parents and extended family). Growing up, examples of unconditional love are also experienced as you care for and receive unconditional love from your pets.

As an adult, parenthood offers another source for learning about unconditional love. Providing life and being responsible for rearing a human being (regardless of their genetic relationship to us) who initially relies on us for their ability to thrive in a healthy and happy manner, we come face-to-face with the sometimes surprising reality of loving another being so completely and unconditionally.

In the end, you alone are responsible for seeking out ways of demonstrating unconditional love, regardless of the extent of your earlier experiences and positive role modeling. Your personal capacity for unconditional love exists on a continuum that is limitless in its attainability. Ultimately, your ability to love without conditions is demonstrated by your capacity to open your heart and simply love, without judgment, ego, vulnerability, or fear. To be unconditionally loving of others would suggest an incredibly evolved human spirit.

Joy

Through joy you find your truth. It is through the experience of simple joys, things you appreciate and are grateful for (like laughing hysterically at the spontaneous humor of someone you love, or sharing a tender moment with your child) that you experience life fully. Experiencing joy in present moment awareness enables you to be joy.

In joy, you harbor no ill feelings, no grief, sadness, loss, or sorrow. You are able to be the incredible being that you are without any reservations or awkwardness but rather with truth and authenticity.

The purpose of finding moments of joy to appreciate is in what they offer us. When you receive joy in your heart, you are likely to share it. It is the moments of joy that you remember fondly, and that remind you of the simplicity of what creates pleasure in life.

Since joy acts as a barometer of truth, your ability to create and experience joy ensues in your search for real love. You cannot possibly be with someone unless you can experience joy in their presence, not because of what they do or say but simply as the result of being with them.

The true measure of joy is to be able to live authentically and honestly in your experience of the world—without worry whether the person you have chosen to be with will understand, appreciate, support, validate, honor, or accept you. To allow yourself to be authentic in your experience of all that is joyful to you in the presence of someone you love infers that they too can share in your experience of truth.

Finding Moments of Joy

Spontaneous moments of joy are often found in the simplest of things. You find your own personal moments of joy when you begin to look for occasions to be yourself and to enjoy what you notice as you remain open to joy.

In seeking out and experiencing joy, you are reminded of all that is good and honorable. It becomes easier for you to be your true self when you are joyful. Sharing your authentic self with others is a natural consequence of experiencing joy.

Reflect on some of your recent sources of joy. Now begin to search out moments in your everyday life when you can appreciate, smile, laugh, and when you can elicit the experience of joy. Record a list here of some of the easy possibilities for finding joy in your life.

I find joy in…

In your love relationship, consider ways in which you can create joyful moments. A spontaneous hug, a thoughtful gesture, or a heartfelt compliment goes a long way to create joy. Consider all of the ways in which you can create joy (for yourself and others) simply by what you say and do that comes from a place of authenticity and sincerity. A healthy love relationship thrives when you consciously seek to create (and receive) joy.

Being in a love relationship that contributes to and enhances the quality of your life makes it easy to experience joy. Your experience of self and your ability to be joyful is not created by your relationship (nor by the person you are in relationship with) but rather from the cumulative effect of what the relationship offers as a complement to allowing yourself to be who you are.

⑃

Kate had been dating Evan for eleven months when she came in to see me. She spoke at length about how Evan had been so incredible (attentive, romantic, thoughtful, and generous) throughout the first eight months of their relationship. After dating for only several weeks, Evan professed his love for Kate, and insisted that he was going to marry her. Kate admitted that she often felt overwhelmed by Evan's repeated proclamations of love. How could

Evan possibly know that she was "the one"? And yet at the same time, hearing these words felt so good.

It was only recently that Kate had began to feel "out of control." Much of their time as a couple was spent in the company of Evan's friends despite Kate's repeated requests to have more one-on-one time. In Evan, Kate also observed a pattern of excessive drinking and a deliberate avoidance of the problems or issues that she would raise. As committed to the relationship as Evan proclaimed to be, he recently admitted to Kate that he "felt overwhelmed" and "could not continue with their relationship right now."

Kate expressed her sadness and confusion. She had wanted the relationship to work so much that she ignored Evan's excessive drinking, did her best to be a part of the weekend parties he hosted, and even tried to figure out what she "could be doing wrong that was causing him to doubt his commitment." When Evan approached her saying he needed to "take a break" to figure things out, and that he would be dating other people as he did this, Kate lost her cool.

With Evan, Kate had felt loved and special, and he seemed to say all of the right things and he made her feel good. Divorced after 14-years of marriage, Kate had been dating for nearly three years before meeting Evan. Kate admitted that she was "not very good" at being on her own. On the weekends that her children were with their father, Kate kept herself busy by seeing friends and going out socially. She admitted feeling lonely without the presence of others.

Evan admitted that he loved the idea of being in love. Making tremendous efforts to woo and win Kate was exciting and exhilarating for him. When Kate finally reciprocated his love and began making plans toward their future, Evan began to back away. He could say the words, "I love you" and make promises of marriage, but on many levels he was afraid to commit fully again to just one woman. Their push and pull relationship had becoming exhausting for Kate.

Before Kate could move on with her own life, she needed to be able to let go of her emotional attachment to Evan, and the idea of what he promised. Kate needed to look at the past eleven months with open eyes in order to critically examine the relationship for what it was, and to accept that Evan was comfortable with the notion of being "in love" but not yet ready for an absolute commitment. Ultimately, he loved his freedom more than he loved Kate. Kate also needed to spend time alone, to love and nurture the person that she is. She needed to believe in herself fully so that she would not have to rely on anyone else for feelings of self-esteem and self-worth.

ℭℨ

When joyful moments with your partner become elusive, or when joy is experienced as a result of doing activities rather than enjoying each other, it is a telling sign that something is very wrong. If the majority of your waking hours is spent investing emotional, mental, and physical energy placating, fixing, or dealing with issues in your love relationship, you need to examine what you are doing. A healthy love relationship should easily evoke joy.

Chapter Six

The Difference Between "Okay" and ... "Incredible!"

What's holding you back from incredible?

If your love relationship has incredible potential, and yet it's not incredible, you need to return to some basics. Most couples who have been in relationship for an extended period of time fall into set patterns and can easily become complacent. It's important to pick up on the subtle cues that suggest attention and effort is needed. Even returning to the small gestures of love and affection that were instinctive at the outset of your relationship goes far in rekindling positive feelings and comfort.

Couples who are committed to their long-term relationship often choose therapy as one way of improving their current status. Having a trained professional assist with tools and techniques that are specific to the issues you want to resolve is a valuable investment of both your time and money. The only caveat here is that you can improve a good relationship only as much as both members of the couple actively seek to do so.

Regardless of the changes that clients achieve, I remind them of the importance of keeping up their positive behaviors. Couples who believe that they have "fixed" their relationship issues breathe a happy sigh of relief and direct their attention to other aspects of life. When a couple stops doing what was working, however, the relationship inevitably returns to its "pre-therapy" state (or in some cases, becomes even worse).

All of the foundational elements listed below and any that I may suggest in the context of a therapy session are included for an important reason. They work, but you need to implement them. Love is not enough to make a good relationship incredible. The idea that your love relationship can exist with little effort or work is a well-established myth. A relationship requires constant attention and effort as it is meant to evolve with time. Your relationship will also present you with personal challenges and opportunities for growth. How you choose to deal with those challenges speaks to the depth of what becomes possible.

An incredible relationship can only exist with such founding elements as: respect, forgiveness, honesty, understanding, and self-esteem. Building an incredible relationship comes with effort and work, and the mutual intention to nurture your relationship, strengthening the depth and devotion of your love. When both members of a couple choose to evolve their individual selves, their love relationship evolves, becoming far more honest, authentic, and complete as a result.

What follows are the necessary elements for making a good relationship incredible. These founding constructs are not new, yet many of us have never fully mastered them. We think we are being respectful or honest, but the truth is we have much work still to do. Like any of the tools and techniques couples learn in the context of a therapy session, you must be able to first apply these to your self. People who have difficulty exemplifying self-respect, love, honesty, understanding, forgiveness, and healthy self-esteem as fundamental human constructs will invariably struggle to be able to offer these to their partner.

In a mutually fulfilling relationship, both partners are conscious of the need to exemplify these constructs as the basis on which their relationship is founded. At any time in your love relationship, return to these elements as a way of adding layers of depth and fulfillment to what is already a "good" relationship. Remember, you can create incredible if you truly want it.

Respect

Respect is one of the cornerstones of a loving and healing relationship. Respect comes in many forms and can be lost as well as rebuilt with effort and a marked change in attitude and behavior. Respect occurs when the two people in a love relationship wholly appreciate and value each other. You outwardly demonstrate respect through your actions. The greater your capacity for self-respect, the easier it is to demonstrate respect for others, particularly your life mate.

Answer the following questions (based on the four categories as indicated) as a personal assessment of the existing mutual respect in your love relationship:

	Always	Often	Occasionally	Seldom
1. I value my partner's opinion and perspective.				
2. I actively demonstrate that I value my partner's opinion and perspective.				
3. I treat my partner with courtesy and respect.				
4. I respect my partner's need to do what is ultimately best for them, acknowledging that it may not always be what I would prefer.				
5. I honor my partner for the person that they are by showing my appreciation of them of them.				
6. I respect my partner's need for privacy and space to be their own individual.				
7. I am respectful of my partner's material property (i.e. personal belongings, possessions)				
8. I am able to show remorse and actively correct my behavior when I am not respectful of my partner.				

Take a closer look at your responses and what they tell you about where respect needs to be built in your relationship. Recognize the difference between behaving improperly out of a momentary mood state, and occasions where you purposefully disrespect your partner.

Fundamental respect of another human being is both learned and developed out of knowledge and wisdom. You behave initially as a result of what you are taught and what you observe growing up in your family of origin. As an adult, you make choices (hopefully with full consciousness) around how you treat others.

With low self-esteem, it is likely that you will display a higher degree of respect towards others than you will for yourself. Self-respect can be elusive to spot. You may believe that you carry a healthy level of self-respect but then relinquish what you believe is right in place of making your partner happy. Allowing your self to be mistreated or taken advantage of is another sign of a lack of self-respect. If you have been taught to sacrifice your needs in favor of your partner's, this perpetuates low self-esteem and sends a message to your partner that their needs are more important—more valuable—than yours.

Respect has multiple forms and meanings. It is most easily given to others when you can first practice it for your self. If you answered "occasionally" or "seldom" to any of the above questions, you need to continue working on your display of respect with your partner (and likely your self-respect needs to be addressed). Being respectful shows that you value and care for the other person. Showing respect goes a long way toward contributing to your greater understanding of each other.

Self-Practice: Respect

You teach others how to treat you. When you consistently allow others to treat you with a lack of respect you are sending the message that you condone their behavior. Particularly at the outset of a new love relationship, but at any time, practice receiving respect by letting your partner know when their words or actions are hurtful or inappropriate. Teach your partner (and others) how you want to be treated by giving a clear example of what they need to do differently. Positively reinforce your partner's appropriate behavior if you want it to continue.

In order to know how you want to be treated, you need to be clear about what "respectful" looks like. To teach others how to treat you means that you respect yourself. The manner in which you behave reflects this.

Your Homework:

Create a list of behaviors that indicate self-respect. These may be things that you have recently begun to do or behaviors that you would like to become better at. Because you now have a list, be committed to examining ways in which you can seek out and practice respectful ways of being.

On another page in your journal, keep a running log of the self-respecting behaviors that you follow through with. Note the positive feelings that are associated with valuing who you are.

Understanding

When you practice understanding, you put aside assumptions and preconceived ideas about what you think you know and instead, seek to learn all that you can. Being understanding is an acquired skill. It requires that you sit back and listen carefully with an open mind. Understanding occurs as you validate what you hear without judgment. When you behave in a way that exemplifies caring and concern, you create a safe environment for your mate to be who they are with authenticity.

Henry and Tia had met at work a few years before they came to see me. At that time, Henry was going through a difficult period as his marriage of four years had recently ended. As Tia and Henry grew closer and eventually began dating, Henry's former wife, Hannah, became very bitter and wrongly accused Tia of breaking up her marriage. In anger, Hannah was determined to make it difficult for Henry to see his eleven-year-old son, Luke.

Henry and Tia eventually married and had a daughter of their own. Henry shared custody of Luke with Hannah, who continued to harbor angry feelings. She spoke badly of Henry to Luke and did her best to portray Tia as the person who ruined their family.

Even as Tia witnessed first hand the constant battle that Henry faced in his efforts to see his son, she was unprepared for her own feelings toward Luke. As she struggled with raising her infant daughter, working shifts, and finding time to be with Henry, Tia began to resent Luke's visits as he seemed to monopolize all of Henry's time. Tia felt threatened. She felt as though Hannah still controlled aspects of her relationship with Henry and dreaded the fact that his ex-wife would always be in their life. Feeling frustrated, Tia presented Henry with an ultimatum—"choose Luke or your new family." Tia forbade Henry to visit with Luke in their home. Even while she knew what she was asking of Henry, Tia did not truly understand what her ultimatum meant.

Without seeking to understand others, you create incredible barriers. Eventually, the two individuals in a love relationship reach an impasse. Without practicing the art of understanding, the barriers that you create may eventually give (Tia ultimately couldn't expect Henry to give up seeing his son), but they leave scars of resentment and anger. Unless Tia found a way to practice compassion and understanding, she would always struggle with her feelings of anger and resentment toward Luke, Hannah, and Henry.

Understanding actually has very little to do with communicating your own thoughts and feelings. When you seek to understand another human being, you put aside your need to speak about your perspective for a moment. Your focus shifts temporarily to one of compassion and empathy. Understanding is about listening. It is about doing your best to hear the message of the other person correctly. In demonstrating understanding you may need to repeat parts or all of the message (as in active listening). The purpose of doing so is to let your partner know that you have heard clearly and completely. Without practicing understanding you become tied up in your own preconceived ideas and assumptions. Even as your intentions may be honorable, your efforts can easily lead to misunderstandings and at times, conflict.

If you "seek to understand" first, there is much less chance of confusion and misinterpretation. Understanding is synonymous with listening and practicing empathy. It doesn't mean that you have to agree or condone someone's behavior, but rather do your best to ensure that you have accurate knowledge of what was communicated. When you seek to understand, your partner can feel supported (even if your opinions differ), and validated in their experience. To understand another human being means that you are able to open yourself up to the experience of listening and hearing without judgment or preconceived assumptions.

In your love relationship, look for opportunities to practice understanding each day.

Self-Practice: Understanding

As you become more skilled at understanding, you will notice that your partner and others (quite naturally) begin to open up and share of themselves more of the time. Understanding simply means listening intently and acknowledging what your heard. Contrary to what you might think, you can be understanding without needing to fix or solve anyone's problems.

Your Homework:

Use active listening to foster your practice of understanding. Listen carefully as your partner is speaking and paraphrase back to them what you heard. Make it easier for yourself by using some of their exact language as you active listen back. Here's an example of what active listening looks like:

Jill: I can't believe my sister didn't call me back. She always seems too busy for me! She says that she really wants to develop a closer relationship with me, but then she does stuff like this. I just don't get it.

David: It must be confusing for you—your sister tells you she wants a closer relationship and then she doesn't return your call.

In the example, David didn't attempt to appease Jill or try and make her feel better. All he did was actively listen to what he heard her say—using empathy.

When your partner makes an effort to actively listen, you feel heard and validated. Hearing your thoughts repeated back to you allows you to contemplate a different perspective. Without active listening, your partner may attempt to offer their opinion or challenge your thoughts. When this occurs, it is likely that you will respond by defending your position, therefore becoming further entrenched in your point of view. Having your thoughts and rationale reflected back to you makes it far easier to rethink or analyze your position and your line of reasoning. In the above example, Jill went on to actually defend her sister. She was able to recognize that her sister being busy meant simply that. It had little to do with not wanting to have a closer relationship.

Jill: Well, she did just start a new full time job. She must be pretty swamped. I think I'll call her and see how she's doing. I really do miss her.

Forgiveness

Gisele came to me in hopes of getting "unstuck." Relying entirely on her courage and inner strength, she left a marriage of more than thirty years to her "high-school sweetheart." Throughout the entire relationship, Gisele had quietly suffered severe emotional and psychological abuse. Walking away from what felt like "a lifetime of being belittled, chastised, and ridiculed," with little but her clothes and some personal belongings, Gisele was finally free. What she soon realized was that she wasn't able to leave behind the emotional scars from years of torment and malevolence.

In spite of her outgoing, positive attitude and vivacious qualities, Gisele had difficulty finding herself. Tormented with self-blame and anger, she became tearful as she relayed how she had longed to even once hear her husband say, "I love you." The costs—emotional, psychological, and spiritual—to Gisele's core self were insurmountable.

What Gisele needed most was to heal from her relationship. Even though she had physically left her husband two years before she came to see me, Gisele still needed to forgive herself for knowingly enduring the abuse (and all of the emotional pain, embarrassment, and loss of self-worth) for so long. To forgive meant that Gisele would first have to acknowledge to herself that the abuse did happen, especially since her ex-husband frequently denied his wrongdoings.

For Gisele, forgiveness needed to begin from within before she would be able to fully go forward in her life.

Forgiveness may need to occur at the end of a love relationship, as a necessity for healing and moving forward. It also needs to be practiced daily as a facet of a healthy love relationship.

Practice forgiveness as a way of letting go of comments and behaviors that hurt even though they were said at times of heightened emotion. Recognize that when your partner says or does something that you perceive as hurtful or insensitive, they may be struggling with their own personal issues in that particular moment. Part of your responsibility is to decide how valuable it is to hold a grudge when words are said that you know don't reflect your partner's true feelings. When you or your partner speak out in moments of escalated tension or personal turmoil, your statements are based on situational thoughts and emotions that are predominantly irrational in nature.

Typically, emotional turmoil experienced by one or both members of a couple reflect an inability to speak honestly and openly about issues and problems. If you are aware of the fact that your partner has a difficult time disclosing their true feelings, you need to check it out. Often there is a great deal more going on beneath the surface.

If you have been in a relationship like Gisele's, where hurtful and pejorative comments had become an everyday occurrence, you need to be able to forgive yourself for continuing to remain in such a toxic environment. For a number of different reasons, you may have decided that you are not able to leave just yet.

Forgiveness on a grand scale occurs every day as you seek out ways in which to be open and loving with your partner. To forgive means that you are not tied to the expectations of what someone should or shouldn't say or do. To forgive means that you do not hold onto mistakes others make. To let go completely means that you have forgiven the person as well as their actions. To forgive requires a full and loving heart.

Understandably, most of us struggle with the concept of forgiveness. We remain imprisoned by our wounded ego and retaliate by judging others unfairly. Holding onto being wronged or hurt, we cannot possibly forgive. We are burdened by our inability to forgive, partly because of the tremendous emotional effort that is involved in staying angry, upset, hurt, or indignant. Losing your need to remain stuck in the past (and bound by your emotional wounds) requires effort and work—and the willingness to want to forgive.

Self-Practice: Forgiveness

Consider all of the incidents for which you harbor resentment and ill will. Think about all of the things you silently haven't forgiven. If you don't tell your mate what they've done or said that you deem "wrong," they can't possibly make amends or change their behavior. The first step to forgiveness on a daily basis is communication. Explain your perspective and how you felt as a result of your partner's words or actions, rather than pointing blame and assuming that they hurt you intentionally.

The purpose of this is to communicate valuable information so that you and your partner can create a better understanding of one another. (You may be surprised to learn that what your partner had said was completely misinterpreted. In this same example, your partner learns the reasons behind why you are sensitive about this particular topic, and this can only help them to understand you better.)

For Gisele (like many others), time was a helpful factor in helping her to forgive herself. The more time that she was on her own, living her life in a way that was healthy and positive, the more her self-worth grew. As she surrounded herself with positive people and experiences, and began focusing on a new career that she had always felt passionate about, Gisele was able to acknowledge how her past abusive relationship was not her fault. It also helped Gisele to recall specific incidents from her previous relationship that continued to haunt her, and to forgive herself, acknowledging acceptance of her behaviors without judgment.

In situations like Gisele's where a relationship has ended, it is not always necessary to forgive the person directly. In regaining feelings of positive self-worth, Gisele was able to forgive her former husband. She could literally "feel the weight lifting" from her chest as she acknowledged situations and events from her past that previously tormented her, and as she felt forgiveness toward her former husband.

Your Homework:

With your current partner, practice regular forgiveness by re-framing the way you perceive events that are hurtful. Analyze the situation from the perspective of your partner. In most cases, your partner has not deliberately sought to behave in a way that would hurt you. Communicate when you feel hurt using "I" statements.

For example, "I felt hurt when..." or "I feel [insert feeling] when...."

Ensure that your dialogue allows you to express the thoughts that have created your feelings. Seek to understand your partner's perspective and to give them an opportunity to right the situation.

Love relationships are not fairy tales. You need to say exactly what you feel in order to be able to work through a problem. (What becomes important is your delivery of the message—how you choose to say what you say.) What allows two people to come together and to move forward from any conflict is their capacity to forgive and their underlying commitment to each other to work through any difficulty and find a healthy solution.

Forgiveness doesn't mean forgetting. Sometimes you need to remember what you or your partner said that might have been the catalyst for an argument. You need to remember so that you can learn from your mistakes and not find yourself in a similar situation because of something that you could have prevented.

To forgive your partner—and you should plan on forgiving repeatedly throughout the course of your love relationship—you need to be willing to love them completely and fully. You need to love and honor your partner, and to value the relationship you have built together, *more than* you are willing to hold a grudge based on their momentarily bad behavior.

Full Frontal Honesty

We give honesty a lot of lip service, but how dedicated to it are we really? How prepared are we to be completely honest with ourselves, and then with those closest to us? How much risk would we take in being fully honest? And would our risk pay off?

When you communicate with honesty, you experience authenticity. What you say is truthfully what you think and feel. There is no incongruence. And yet, most of us are cautious about sharing our most intimate thoughts and feelings with full frontal honesty. As children, we start out speaking openly and truthfully and over time learn what not to say, or what we shouldn't say, or choose not to speak if our thoughts and feelings are invalidated in some way.

As adults, we often choose to say what we think our partner wants to hear, what we know they would agree with, or we say little at all. But later, when we are struggling with what we really want and if we choose to voice our real feelings, our partner is surprised, confused, or hurt. It isn't that we necessarily lied, but we didn't really speak the truth either.

Honesty is one of the few things that facilitates communication and builds trust. Sharing your thoughts and feelings with honesty means that you will become better at expressing yourself. To know that your partner will always tell you exactly what they think and feel (even if they have to be gentle with the delivery of what they are saying) is the cornerstone to authenticity and trust. Your partner needs to be the one person (at the very least) that you can be completely yourself with, and this includes sharing your honest thoughts and opinions.

If you haven't yet figured out how to be honest with yourself, it becomes almost impossible to be honest in your love relationship. Self-honesty starts with acknowledging your inner thoughts and opinions as real and important. Listening to yourself, and following through with what you believe is right is an integral practice to developing self-honesty.

Ultimately, you need to remember that your ideas and views will differ from others. Rather than seek to comply or unite with the majority, self-honesty is simply the expression of your point of view. This is also your chance to learn about others' point of view.

Self-Practice: Honesty

Take a moment to think about what your personal opinion is when asked. Begin by sharing small messages of honesty about topics and situations you feel most comfortable (and safe) speaking about. As you build your confidence, you may decide to revisit statements and opinions you previously made, clarifying and revising these to reflect how you honestly feel. In a healthy love relationship, you will feel safe and supported to express yourself truthfully, and to explain your desire to practice honesty all of the time.

Your Homework:

If your partner is not used to hearing you speak honestly, your comments may be confusing and perceived as coming "out of left field." As you make the commitment to practice honesty with yourself and others, let your partner know that this is what you will be doing. Challenge yourself to communicate, even at times when you find it difficult to do so. Use any or all of the following sentence stems as a way of letting your partner (and others) know that you are speaking your truth:

For example:

"As difficult as it is to be honest ..."

"If I am completely honest then I would have to say ..."

"You may not agree with my opinion, but to respond honestly ..."

Notice how you feel every time that you speak honestly. Notice what happens to your self-esteem every time that you honor, and voice, what you believe to be the truth.

Self-Esteem

Your self-esteem is at the core of how you think, feel, and behave, affecting every aspect of your existence. Your level of healthy self-esteem affects your ability to feel worthy of happiness and to cope with the ongoing challenges of life. The greater your level of healthy self-esteem—the value and worth you place on yourself and your abilities—the greater your confidence in knowing your self and what you want from a love relationship. With healthy self-esteem, it is much easier to be authentic in your love relationship.

Self-esteem is measured as the way in which you think and feel about yourself, your level of confidence in being able to meet challenges and new experiences, and your belief in your ability to thrive and succeed when faced with minor (or major) setbacks. Your self-esteem exists on a continuum based on cumulative life experiences, how are you socialized, and your personal belief system. Your level of healthy self-esteem moves from left to right along a continuum, growing as you seek new challenges and as you experience positive events and personal success.

The development of self-esteem begins early in life through praise and the experience of positive success (i.e. learning how to swim or getting good grades at school). When parents and other caregivers instill and support positive self-esteem, children grow up well equipped to seek out (and embrace) situations, experiences, and challenges in which they can continue to build their confidence and self-esteem. Even as they experience setbacks these are often offset with encouragement and the desire to improve in order to "do better" next time. With consistent reinforcement of their self-esteem, children become confident, self-assured, independent young adults. From here, they are able to continue growing healthy self-esteem throughout their life.

Self-esteem is also established out of a sense of feeling loved and accepted. As a child in your family of origin, feeling the love that comes from knowing you are supported and encouraged to grow and to become the very best that you can, helps to foster healthy self-esteem.

With a healthy level of self-esteem you feel confident to share your real self with others. Your level of self-esteem allows you the confidence to be who you are without fear of rejection or criticism. Because you believe in yourself and your abilities, healthy self-esteem allows you to overcome obstacles as you pursue and achieve your goals. You feel better equipped to deal with life issues – as well as the various internal struggles that you face as you challenge what you may have been taught to believe – choosing instead what you believe is right based on new information you have learned, your education, and your life experiences. The higher your self-esteem, the greater your desire for finding a partner that is most compatible with you.

Building healthy self-esteem is something that you continue to do throughout your lifetime. The higher your authentic self-esteem, the easier it is to focus outside of yourself, seeing the challenges others' face, and to be empathetic and compassionate toward them. With low self-esteem, you struggle with critical self-doubt, confidence, and emotional independence, causing you to remain self-focused. It is far more difficult to look outside of yourself, to be present in your life, and to enjoy present moments because you are caught up in the apprehension and anxiety created in part from low levels of self-esteem.

Self-Practice: Self-Esteem

You can increase your existing level of self-esteem. Using a journal or notebook, answer the following questions, leaving room to add additional responses over time. Self-esteem grows exponentially as a result of the work that you do to build it.

1. Identify your value and self-worth. (i.e. What do you believe about yourself to be true? What aspects of yourself, do you most value and appreciate? What are your strengths? What are you able to offer others that they come to you for help?)

2. Develop a list of positive core attributes and abilities. How do you define yourself? List all of the qualities that describe who you are. Ensure that you create this list at a time when you are in positive mood state, as your mood affects how you view yourself.

3. How do you envision yourself to be? (e.g. Important to growing healthy self-esteem is identifying aspects of your-self that you want to improve.) Your willingness to want more from yourself (to not accept "good enough") means that you are likely to work on those aspects, even seeking help at times to do so. Your commitment to achieving more from yourself means that you are much more likely to at-tain this. Creating successes in your development of self fur-ther builds confidence and self-esteem.

4. Even more important then what happens to you is what you do with what happens to you. Consider how you view events and situations in your life. Important for nurturing healthy self-esteem is your ability to examine situations with a proactive position, rather than feeling powerless. Instead, work to create a positive outcome and look for the life les-sons that are inherent in all events.

5. Cultivate a regular practice of self-care behaviors. To grow healthy self-esteem, you need to behave in a loving way to-ward your self. (This includes being mindful of your self-talk.) Regardless of whether you received unconditional love growing up, you need to learn how to love and accept yourself unconditionally. This is paramount to achieving healthy self-esteem and positive self-worth. To do this, cre-ate a list of behaviors and activities that contribute to your positive sense of self. Ensure that you honor these, as a way of reinforcing your value and worth on a daily basis.

Your Homework:

Create a list of positive qualities that you ascribe to. These are elements that you need to begin working on in order to raise your level of self-esteem. Using your answers from Item 3 above, identify the specific personality traits, behaviors, and qualities that you want to develop as your own. Consider working with a professional therapist if you want to learn healthy strategies for exploring your past in order to gain a better understanding of yourself, to change old patterns of behaving, or to challenge problematic core beliefs.

As an adult, only you can raise your self-esteem. Using your detailed list, begin working on the items that are easiest to accomplish first. Create and complete action steps for these to help move you closer to attaining your goals. As you achieve a goal, begin working on the next one. This becomes a life list since you may need to work on the development of some qualities longer than others, and as you continue to ascribe to wanting more for yourself.

Having healthy self-esteem means that you value and appreciate the person that you are. It means that you are unwilling to sacrifice your goals and dreams for others and that you remain committed to fulfilling what is most important to you. Healthy self-esteem continues to develop out of your personal successes, rather than those of your spouse, children, or members in your family of origin. Authentic self-esteem is not based on material possessions, money, or ego.

In your love relationship, having healthy self-esteem means that you are able to give of yourself to your partner without expecting the same, or more, in return. Because you feel confident in who you are and in your abilities, you are self-sufficient, emotionally independent, and confident in your day-to-day decisions. With healthy self-esteem you feel able to succeed in your life. You feel equipped to create and achieve goals that are important to you as an individual. Self-esteem enables you to act with freedom of choice.

Expectations

One of the more challenging, and yet unexamined, elements of a healthy love relationship is the ability to let go of the unrealistic expectations you place on yourself and your partner. Fundamental to letting go is recognizing when the expectations you hold are unreasonable.

When you place expectations on your partner and on your love relationship, you are inherently saying that what you have and whom you are with is not good enough. Expectations are unwritten rules that you live by that originate from your core beliefs. Your expectations are based on the way you believe something "should" be. "Should" implies that something is occurring (or not occurring) that needs to be different. For example, perhaps you have always expected yourself to provide an affluent lifestyle for your family, but then extreme changes in the market dictate a drastic cut in your salary as a stockbroker. Your core belief has shaped your view that your personal success and self-worth are based on your earning potential. How does this sudden and unexpected life event affect the expectations that you hold for yourself?

In a different example, as a result of your previous partner's multiple infidelities, you have decided that you need to always be attractive and sexually available in order to keep your partner satisfied (and to keep his eyes from wandering). Your expectation is largely tied to your core belief of needing to be "good enough" in order to feel loved, appreciated, and desired.

Consider what some of your expectations are. Consider what expectations you firmly hold for your partner and for the relationship. Identify these below.

My Expectations ...

for myself	for my mate	for my love relationship

Next, consider the following:

Do any of your self-imposed expectations create unnecessary pressure? What would it mean if you were to give these up?

Which expectations tend to create conflict between you and your mate? These are the expectations that you need to examine carefully. What are they based on? How realistic are they? How successful is your mate in meeting (or exceeding) your expectations?

Have you verbalized your expectations of your mate? If so, how were they received?

If your expectations are unrealistic, it is unlikely that they can ever be successfully achieved. Challenge your expectations in the same way that you would challenge your core beliefs. (e.g. Where's the evidence that my self-worth and personal success is dependent on earning a certain level of income? It may be one aspect of how you decide you want to view yourself, but it is certainly not the only factor on which to base your self-worth.) Be conscious of the inherent flaws in your belief system so that you can choose to set reasonable expectations instead. Because most of your expectations will be unrealistic and erroneous, continuing to hold them means that you continue to set yourself (and others) up to fail. You can't possibly feel good about yourself or your relationship when your expectations reflect an unreasonable or impossible task.

In contrast, having expectations that have to do with your becoming better in some way can be wholly inspiring. For example, to expect that you will continue to challenge your thoughts in moments when you feel angry—in order to gain better control over your reactions—is a reasonable goal that you can actively work toward.

൪

In love relationships, unreasonable expectations set you up to feel disappointed, annoyed, anxious, hurt, jealous, and angry—especially if your unrealistic expectations surround situations that occur on a regular basis. Holding unrealistic expectations of what you deem is appropriate, right, proper, reasonable, "must happen," or "should be" is like having the only copy of a secret playbook. The other players can't possibly make the plays you are expecting because they simply don't know them.

Communicate your expectations with your partner—even if you have never done so before. Having an open and honest dialogue about your expectations enables you as a couple to establish some healthy ground rules. If you silently hold onto your expectations—however minor they may be—you set yourself, and your partner, up to fail.

Holding unrealistic expectations makes it difficult for your partner to ever succeed based on your standards. The net result is a low level of resentment within you that builds over time, causing you to become annoyed and intolerant of their behavior.

To let go of unrealistic expectations that you hold about yourself or others you need to be consciously aware of the inner dialogue that reaffirms and perpetuates these ideas. Catch yourself as you rehearse what you say in moments when you are placing expectations on yourself or others. Challenge your expectations as you would your inner thoughts. Use "Where's the evidence?" on your current expectations to challenge how reasonable they really are. Be prepared to create new, accurate expectations for the relationship, and each other, that you both agree on, and which come out of your open dialogue.

Holding pre-conceived expectations of how you believe things "should be," keeps you from experiencing "what is." Instead, practice being open and accepting of what your partner, and the relationship, is able to offer at this moment. If you believe that something different needs to happen, it's up to you to communicate that. Whether or not your expectation is shared is not as important as what you and your partner do to communicate your respective thoughts and feelings in order to figure out a suitable solution. When you are prepared to renegotiate the unrealistic expectations that you hold for yourself and your partner, you are then able to let these go in place of a far healthier way of operating.

What About Sex?

While only some of the couples that I see talk about their life in the bedroom, the sexual relationship of a couple is actually a good barometer of the relationship's overall success. How you experience yourself as a sexual being and the degree to which you can express yourself via your sexual behavior and shared intimacy is reflected in the overall health of the relationship.

Paying attention to the sexual and intimacy needs of your love relationship is crucial on many levels.

Sex and intimacy (romantic kissing, tenderness, touching, and closeness) is the primary method by which two people can explicitly, and exclusively, share their selves with each other. Being sexual with your partner is the one thing that you reserve specifically for that person.

Going outside of your relationship (whether openly, with your partner's agreement, or as in an affair) for some form of sexual experience, changes the sacred element of what you and your partner have established. Feeling confined or trapped by the social mores or institutionalized rules of your love relationship and needing to explore sex and intimacy desires with people other than your partner, suggests that you, on some level, desire more than your current relationship offers. The moment that one or both members of a couple go outside of the love relationship for sex, regardless of the agreement or reason, the sanctity of the relationship is forever changed.

Like other elements of the couple relationship, sexual practice and behavior need attention and effort. Common examples of reoccurring issues in a couple's sexual relationship include: infrequency of sex or sexual intimacy, a lack of sexual satisfaction (inability to meet one's needs for emotional or physical intimacy), and limited healthy sexual experimentation or creativity, all of which are exacerbated by a lack of communication.

On a fundamental level, women and men perceive sex as an element of a love relationship differently. Regardless of sexual orientation, women typically require an emotional connection with their mate prior to being sexual. Experiencing a sense of connection on an emotional level with someone means that women are then more easily able to share themselves sexually with that person. Men typically do not need the same level of emotional connection in order to be sexual. For men, having sex is what allows them to feel emotionally connected to their partner; sex is the antecedent for an emotional connection. Typically, the two people in relationship have opposing (yet, often unspoken) needs. When clients discuss issues surrounding sexual frequency or satisfaction, they often don't realize the very different requirements that exist for each gender.

A couple who said that they were "high-school sweethearts," Kevin and Adriana decided to pursue counseling as a way of re-connecting in the bedroom. While Kevin raised the subject of sex since he was feeling frustrated with the lack of spontaneity and fre-quency of their current sex life, Adriana (a stay-at-home mother of three children under the age of six) was struggling with the stresses that came with attempting to juggle the roles of wife, mother, and the many of the day-to-day responsibilities of running a household. Adriana also admitted to feeling growing resentment since she was the one who had given up her job in finance in order to be the pri-mary caregiver. Now, at age 36, Adriana's identity was largely tied up in being a mom. Her dreams of returning to her executive ca-reer seemed far away.

In our session, Adriana admitted that sex was last on her list of priorities, largely because she didn't feel connected with Kevin. When the couple did manage to "arrange" a time to have sex, it became another "task" that Adriana felt pressured to do, since she resented Kevin for not giving her emotional support. In addition to working long hours, Kevin also traveled regularly with his job, spending little time at home to help Adriana with the children. As a result, Adriana found it a challenge to want to have sex.

For Kevin and Adriana—and for many couples who have been together a long time—sex can reach a stalemate. Neither partner was willing to make attempts to meet the other's needs because they both felt wronged by not receiving what they want. Even though Adriana explained that she could feel more romantic if Kevin would take the initiative some nights to draw a bath for her and put the children to bed, Kevin rarely did this. He had given up making this effort since Adriana would often claim to be "too tired" after her bath to have sex.

Kevin had now stopped initiating sex since Adriana repeatedly turned him down. As resentments regarding their sex life remained largely unspoken, Adriana and Kevin's true sentiments would sur-face whenever they became enmeshed in a bitter argument. When-ever either of them became immersed in their personal wounds, each would lash out with hurtful comments. Sex became a weapon rather than a means of expressing and experiencing love. As much as Adriana fantasized about having an active sex life, she needed to feel connected to Kevin and couldn't when he was rarely around. Kevin disclosed that he would make a greater effort to be home if Adriana made some time for the two of them. To Kevin, being home often meant that Adriana would "dump a week's worth of chores" on him. Kevin wanted to be able to connect with his wife, but had given up trying.

Unfortunately Adriana and Kevin's love relationship would continue to deteriorate unless they began to recognize that they needed to share the responsibility for making an effort. Both needed to give as well as receive.

In cases where couples report a lack of spontaneity or sexual creativity and where there was previously a healthy expression of sexual behavior, the solution often lies in refocusing attention on their sexual needs. During hectic or stressful periods, couples (and certainly couples with infants and young children) experience a natural decline in sexual activity that requires effort to combat.

While pregnancy and child rearing add a dimension of challenge to a couples' sexual relationship, most if not all couples naturally experience phases in which less energy and attention is given to the sexual relationship. Ideally there is some honest communication that happens at the outset of this change rather than one or both partners quietly feeling dissatisfied and resentful.

As much as sex is a "couple experience," it is quite common for clients to address problems with their sex life in the context of individual therapy. Janet, a 38-year-old mother of three young boys had begun individual counseling to explore a reoccurring dream specific to a co-worker taunting her about her sexuality. As we began to deconstruct various elements of the dream and examine its symbolism, Janet candidly admitted that she had never experienced an orgasm either with her husband (her only sexual partner) or during masturbation.

The more comfortable you are with your body and in the creating the experience of orgasm, the easier it is to communicate to your partner what you enjoy. Janet revealed that she had very limited experience in exploring her own body. While sex was something that she "participated in," Janet did not know what it was like to experience a heightened sense of pleasure as a sexual being.

In a love relationship, both people will have different needs and desires for sex at different times. It is, therefore, very important that a couple develops a practice of talking openly about their sexual relationship, both when it is fulfilling and when it is not. Feeling embarrassed, afraid, or refusing to address the topic of sex (out of resentment, anger, or indifference) only makes the issue grow.

Creating opportunities to experience intimacy and closeness in addition to sex means making these a priority. Like other elements of a love relationship, sex needs to be an ongoing priority. Being committed to open and honest communication means talking about the real issues underlying the sexual relationship. If the sexual behavior has changed in some way, there needs to be an immediate conversation about what else is going on in your lives that could be contributing to the change.

CR

At times it may feel as though your love relationship has derailed—as if things have come unraveled in some way. Of course, this doesn't happen overnight. When things are going well in the relationship, most couples direct their attention elsewhere. We begin to pay attention again when things aren't working.

When problems initially arise, most couples first avoid or ignore the issues. They rationalize, find excuses, and hope that things can quickly return to a state of equilibrium. This continues indefinitely, or until the problems escalate to a point where they can no longer tolerate it. Conflict typically ensues.

The unstated secret is continual, effective communication. Begin speaking about what you honestly feel, with respect and the desire to understand. Rather than wait until you are furious with your partner, talk about the little things that bother you: little things become big things over time. It makes good sense to remember that the little things are easier to figure out and resolve. Because the big things have taken months or years to develop, chances are that you and your partner have accumulated a history of strong feelings that have affected how you currently feel toward each other.

Return to these core elements as a way of nurturing and strengthening love. The ideal is to integrate these concepts as daily life practices. When both you and your partner actively practice honesty, respect, understanding, forgiveness, sex, and a personal lifelong commitment to growing healthy self-esteem, you have all of the elements in place for happiness and longevity in your relationship—assuming that you have chosen each other wisely.

Chapter Seven

Is It Really Forever?

Is it possible to find the great love of your life ... and if so ...
can it really last for a lifetime?

Today, the notion of living happily ever after is most commonly found at the end of certain, highly romanticized, bedtime fairy tales. Current statistics in North America suggest that between 40 and 55 percent of marriages are likely to end in divorce.

Perhaps the more compelling question is: Are we failing at marriage, or are we entering into a long-term commitment with very little understanding of who we are and what we want from life?

Ponder these questions for a moment ...

• Do we marry (or move in together) with full consciousness and clearly defined goals and intentions for our happiness, or do we hold onto idealistic fantasies of what the perfect love relationship ought to be and assume that our mate will easily fit into our template for a perfect companion?

• Have we considered what our definitions and ideals of marriage are?

• If marriage is another form of "long-term love relationship" how do the religious and legal elements give it any more of a permanent guarantee for longevity and happiness?

Are we really failing at marriage or is it possible that we haven't learned enough about our self first?

Don't All Good Things Come to An End?

As a couple formalizes their mutually exclusive commitment to be in relationship together, they generally do so with hopeful aspirations. Yet, without respectful compassion, the ability for self-awareness and growth, and the necessary "tools" to successfully navigate through the inevitable relationship "road bumps," there is little guarantee that love will flourish and endure.

To love another human being so deeply and unselfishly requires that you remain committed to your own self-evolution and personal growth. It requires that you learn how to move beyond the limits of the material, physical world in which you live and to practice openness of heart and spirit. To love with clarity and truth means that you remain honest with yourself at all times. To remain honest with yourself means that you will choose to end (or support the ending of) a relationship that is no longer supporting your desire to be authentic and whole.

In many cases (I want to say "most," but that would truly be discouraging), couples are really not meant to be together forever. While western society does a great job of promoting and reinforcing the fantasy ideal of the everlasting love relationship, many individuals (if they could allow themselves complete honesty) would admit that they have remained in relationship long after the time their emotional and spiritual growth as a couple has been completed.

Because the majority of the world is still tied to customary cultural and societal rules for love, we believe that the ending of a love relationship is a failure in some way. As such, we are far less inclined to examine what an ending means for our personal growth and our search for a more suitable partner. When a love relationship ends, we rarely practice self-forgiveness, acceptance, or even contentment. We hope to arrive at these compassionate ideals at some later point, but in the meantime, we remain caught up in the overwhelming sense of loss to our own self.

If we remain conscious throughout our love relationship, we will know and anticipate its ending. If we could avoid the fault-finding and absolve the guilt that typically occurs at the end of a relationship, how much more likely would we be to move forward with our whole self intact?

In truth, love relationships are not always meant to last forever. They are meant to teach us important lessons about our self, others, and the world. Our love relationships allow us to heal and to become more whole. When a love relationship has ended, it is because the couple is no longer compatible.

Couples who remain in relationship even though they have completed their purpose for being together have often resigned themselves to staying together for any number of reasons (e.g. not wanting to "break up the family for the sake of their children," guilt, unwillingness to "admit failure," the loss of their economic comfort, or simply because it would be unfamiliar and scary to be single and on their own). In cases where couples remain together and where the relationship does not continue to evolve and grow, they have chosen, whether consciously or unconsciously, to inhibit their personal evolution and capacity for spiritual authenticity. Both members of a couple may find other hobbies, pastimes, friendships, or even partners to fill the void that arises when a love relationship has died. Remaining together when their relationship has completed its purpose leaves the two individuals wedged in a state of unrest. Neither can fully move forward in their own life without first liberating their self from each other.

Amy and Matt were an extreme example of two people who remained together long after they had become spiritually incompatible. Currently in their mid thirties, they had been in relationship together for most of the last 14 years. (On two occasions they had "broken-up" and dated other people.)

In describing the volatility of their arguments, Amy admitted that she "was evil" with Matt. Amy described herself as being "extremely angry," and admitted that her rage would escalate uncontrollably whenever they experienced a conflict. As much as Amy wanted to "stop being so angry all of the time," she was deeply lodged in her past. As long as she continued to blame Matt for all of his past mistakes (including things that were beyond his control), Amy would always be ruled by her anger.

A year before they sought my help, Matt had suffered a serious accident while at work and was currently on disability leave. His back injury meant that he would need to retrain for a different career. Amy blamed Matt for the unexpected change in their financial situation. In a fit of violent rage during a recent argument, Amy had punched Matt in the back repeatedly as she swore obscenities, blaming him for the accident.

In our second session together, Matt spoke of how Amy would pack his bags, placing them at the front door every time they had a fight. As much as Amy wanted Matt to leave, she couldn't bear the thought of him being with anyone else. Amy also wanted to continue living the quality of life that she was used to, which meant that she would need Matt's financial help even if his disability payments were a far cry from what he previously earned.

Matt admitted that he was no longer in love with Amy. The ongoing verbal, emotional, and physical abuse were repeated reminders of all that was wrong with their relationship. Matt confessed that he could not remember when the relationship had become so bad, but only that it was never completely loving and respectful. As much as he knew that walking out meant that he would never come back to Amy, Matt also felt responsible for supporting her and for ensuring that she could still continue to live and work in the house. Matt also felt guilty for causing Amy so much grief. He told himself that he "should be able to make her happy and not angry." In many ways, Matt admitted to feeling somehow responsible for the way in which Amy treated him. He believed that if only he could provide her with what she needed, Amy would have no reason to be so angry all of the time. Unfortunately, Amy and Matt continued to remain emotionally hostage to each other, based on their feelings of guilt, insecurity, anger, and fear.

When a couple has so much history together, living in the past becomes emotional torture. When one or both members of a couple are unwilling or incapable of letting go of past hurts and practicing forgiveness (of their self and their partner), the relationship will inevitably deteriorate.

Amy needed to work on her longstanding reaction of anger (one partially learned from her father who, according to Amy, was a more severe version of herself) and to develop her identity without Matt. Blaming Matt for everything that was wrong in their relationship meant that Amy abdicated any responsibility for her own behaviors. Matt needed to believe that he deserved to be in a healthy and respectful relationship. He needed a partner who could support his challenge to find a new career and to help him succeed by being positive—not by eradicating his self-esteem with cruel and hurtful statements.

Like Amy and Matt, it is rare for your first serious love relationship to be the right one for the rest of your life. Enter into your initial love relationships with the knowledge that each will bring you many positive experiences, and that each experience will bring you closer to figuring out what your ideal is. Part of the inherent learning in a love relationship is in recognizing, and knowing when your relationship has run its course. The ending of a love relationship only becomes more trying and difficult as you ignore what you already know—that it is time to move on.

CB

In contemplating the ending of a love relationship, your biggest question is whether or not the emotional, spiritual, and physical connection continues to exist. Another important factor in your decision is whether you can honestly say that you continue to be a better person for remaining in your relationship. Becoming a better person is something that you personally create, although you ideally receive support, encouragement, and inspiration from your partner to do so. This is different from being dependent on your mate. If your main rationale for saving the relationship is to avoid a change in living standards, to continue having someone take care of you, to prevent your mate from being with someone else, or because you "wouldn't know how to go on" without them, know that all of these are self serving reasons based out of ego or fear.

After a couple of months of working independently with Matt (who decided that he wanted to pursue individual counseling in order to help him with his decision to leave the relationship), he came home one day to find his belongings strewn on the front lawn of their home. It was at this point that he "realized this was it." He immediately gathered his personal possessions and left, knowing that he would be able to do so for good this time.

Matt has since found an apartment, leaving everything including the house itself, to Amy. In the short time that he has been on his own, Matt expressed feeling "free" and a sense of "peacefulness" that replaces the pounding in his chest that he had experienced every day for a very long time. For Matt, this was a way to leave the relationship feeling good within himself. He has since received a generous settlement as compensation for his work injury and is excitedly planning the rest of his life.

CR

As difficult (and inconvenient) as it might be to venture on without the comfort of your love relationship, you can't possibly experience the fullness of your life as long as you remain stifled by fear and dependency. All that is required for you to persevere on your own is the belief that you will survive beyond the ending of your relationship, and that you are willing to develop and build strength of character. As you begin to experience a sense of personal competency, you come to appreciate your autonomy and the eventual realization that you can have a loving and respectful relationship with another human being.

Conversely, if your love relationship offers the support and encouragement for you to continue to grow as an individual, if it continues to honor what you need even as you change and evolve over time, and if you are able to experience and share real love, then it is likely that your relationship is not ready to be over.

Navigating through the Rough Spots

Rough spots exist to remind you that your relationship is fallible. Without the mutual willingness to truly understand each other, couples continue to make assumptions and preconceived notions about what each other really thinks or feels. Since it seems invariably easier to avoid speaking honestly on certain issues, couples get caught in the pattern of doing what they have always done (e.g. remain quiet, become passive-aggressive, manipulate in order to get their way, and so on), without paying attention to the negative impact their behaviors have on their partner and the health of the relationship. To create and maintain a healthy love relationship requires work. Until it feels reasonably comfortable to communicate honestly and candidly, the inevitable rough spots will remain a difficult challenge.

All relationships experience their share of rough spots and with good reason. These point you directly to what needs to be fixed, and in examining the problems you and your partner can strive to uncover the real issues. Couples who say that they never argue often don't reveal their true thoughts and feelings to each other either. Avoiding potential conflict by never speaking about what is bothering you, not being completely truthful about what the real issue is, or avoiding past unresolved issues, is not the most successful way to create a stronger relationship.

The longer a couple exists in a state of quiet distress, the more difficult it becomes to break down the invisible barricade that they have built between them. While the foremost issue that couples bring to therapy is that of communication, oddly enough, most couples aren't saying enough to each other. When there is an opportunity to speak honestly about a particular issue, both members of a couple often dilute their actual thoughts and feelings by saying what they think will be received well or what they can say without creating conflict. Not being completely truthful may save you from a further discussion (or disagreement) right now, but in the long run your mate will be stunned to learn, for example, that you really do want children.

In addition to a lack of honesty and an unwillingness to face issues head on—not for the purpose of creating conflict but to address problems as they come about—rough spots in a love relationship exist when a couple stops encouraging and supporting each other to grow and evolve. The unintentional complacency results in a plateau. Somehow, the earlier concerted effort to appreciate and care for each other has given way to other things: a return to old habits or ways of being, a focus or distraction onto something else, or the simple assumption that love is enough to endure and so attention and effort is momentarily diverted elsewhere.

Couples who make their way to my office often do so as a last resort. Therapy is still perceived as a way of receiving help when things have been wrong for some time and only after a couple claims to have repeatedly exhausted efforts to improve their relationship without achieving the results they want.

Monty and Julia had been married for fifteen years. Their son, Aaron, was eleven. Monty confessed that since Aaron was born, he and Julia no longer had a normal love relationship. Monty explained that Julia was not affectionate with him, nor did she make any efforts to show love. While Julia acted lovingly towards Aaron, Monty, who claimed he required a great deal of nurturing, felt neglected and ignored. Monty and Julia rarely had sex and Julia admitted that she "wasn't really into it."

Monty described feeling frustrated and angry at the lack of effort on Julia's part to become more loving and to do more things together (e.g. walks, dinners out, seeing a movie) as a couple. After several attempts at verbalizing his mounting irritation and disappointment, Monty reported that he had "given up." He retreated, sleeping on the couch, and avoiding Julia whenever possible.

As much as Julia admitted that she was "at fault" for the lack of romance and quality time as a couple, she did little to change anything. Monty avoided communicating his real thoughts and feelings, including his growing anger, and instead vacillated between lecturing Julia on what she was doing wrong and giving up in silent retreat. Keeping themselves busy in their respective jobs, raising their son, and caring for two sets of aging parents, Monty and Julia were going nowhere fast. Creating a better relationship would mean that both would need to make a different kind of effort with each other. Without the right immediate action, their relationship would continue to deteriorate.

ॐ

An inherent challenge in all long-term love relationships is the fact that you accumulate an ever-growing history, not all of which is helpful for some of your present-day issues. Because of your history together, both you and your partner have the ability to recall, and often be consumed by, past experiences that have created intense, painful emotions. For example, you may feel sad and hurt when you think about what your loved one said many years earlier during a particular argument. During a disagreement you recall the previous incident yet again. As you remind your partner of it, it exacerbates your present emotions, and you overreact. You have allowed your relationship history to negatively affect your present.

The longer you remain in relationship with your partner, the greater the likelihood that you bring up emotionally difficult past events and experiences, reacting to them all over again, in present-day. Reliving these past experiences creates conflict and inner turmoil—otherwise known as "emotional rough spots." These sensitive areas stir up an avalanche of emotions, usually out of context to what the real issue is. Instead of assessing each situation separately, you react to a present-day problem with the emotional intensity of a past issue.

While you cannot change the past, you can choose whether your past continues to affect your present. For many couples who find themselves feeling confused and saddened by the fact that they have landed in a place where all that they seem to do is argue and fight, leaving the past behind (unless they are examining a particular issue for the purpose of creating a positive resolution) is one of the first things that they need to do.

What gives strength and longevity to a relationship is the love and respect that two people have for each other. They appreciate that their bond is solid and sacred, and they consistently work to-ward maintaining it. The relationship grows and evolves in a healthy way as long as each partner is also able to individually nurture and evolve their own self, as well as to help the other grow on an emotional, spiritual, psychological, and physical level. A love relationship has a greater potential to withstand the rough spots when both partners are individually inspired to be more.

At the beginning of a new relationship, we simply don't contemplate the thought of rough spots. And yet, relationships are never static. Every life event that you experience has the ability to affect your relationship. Your love relationship requires the attention, energy, and effort of a living thing. Taking your relationship for granted means that you will be less prepared for the rough spots.

ఴ

Although almost completely invisible to the naked eye, the emotional rough spots that Monty and Julia had quietly endured for several years had greatly damaged their relationship. Even while Monty begged Julia to attend couples counseling, it was a long time before she agreed to do so. As much as he worked hard to create opportunities for positive experiences as a couple, Julia seemed to pull herself further and further away from the relationship. Monty made efforts to practice communicating his thoughts and feelings openly, and without lecturing. Julia agreed to go on the occasional "date night" with Monty, but otherwise kept her distance. After several months of feeling exasperated by his efforts to rebuild their relationship, Monty confronted Julia with the idea of separating. To his surprise and dismay, Julia agreed. She confessed that she did not think she could ever be happy with Monty and felt miserable at the thought of spending the rest of her life in this relationship.

Julia only voiced some of what would have likely been years of ongoing unhappiness. The truth was, every time that Monty retreated, avoiding Julia rather than communicating what was wrong, the more Julia blamed herself for the problems in their relationship.

Julia's ongoing struggle with depression (diagnosed several years earlier) was difficult for Monty to understand as a causal factor in her inability to be more affectionate and to do things as a couple. Julia admitted that she had tried for years to understand Monty and to be a loving wife, but every time that he lectured or chastised her, she experienced a wave of self-loathing thoughts and emotions that seemed to bring back all of Monty's previous unresolved complaints. Not having the ability to dialogue effectively about her inner thoughts and feelings, Julia could barely tolerate her life anymore. Monty and Julia eventually went their separate ways.

Ending Points

Even as your relationships have the propensity to teach you a great deal about yourself and others, most are not destined to exist forever. As difficult as it may be to recognize when you are at an ending point, if you do not let go your love relationship can hold you back from the unfinished work that you need to complete.

When a love relationship has ended, there is the potential to learn important life lessons, and for continued personal, spiritual growth. A break-up or divorce happens when you have fulfilled a particular purpose for being in relationship. Long before the physical separation takes place, you become emotionally and spiritually incompatible. Both members of a couple disconnect or separate on an emotional, intellectual, and psychological level. In a relationship that has come to an end even though the partners physically remain in it, each person has already begun to move in different directions.

Vicki and Ben were two people who had completed their destiny as a couple. They had been married for thirty-three years when Vicki first came to see me. She was a retired schoolteacher who, at fifty-four, had an unusually youthful quality about her. While Vicki consciously contained her incredible enthusiasm for life, it would often show itself through her large gestures and animated facial expressions, particularly as she spoke about topics that she felt most passionate about.

Vicki described the inner turmoil that she was attempting to quietly resolve. For years, she had been unhappy in her relationship with Ben. She spoke of having a "good" marriage, yet there appeared to be some very important elements missing.

When Vicki was truthful with herself, she admitted that she had never felt a deep connection with her husband. She described how very different the two of them were. From their diverse interests, communication styles, and even the way in which they approached lovemaking, Vicki painted a picture of two individuals who seemed to be almost polar opposites. When their three daughters were young, both Vicki and Ben seemed to be able to carry off their role as a couple. Both were busy in their individual careers, raising their family, and pursuing (albeit separate) outside activities and interests.

Three years earlier, Vicki and Ben had both retired. Having more time together without the distractions of other responsibilities and commitments made it blatantly clear that Vicki and Ben had "outgrown" each other. Vicki began to realize that her needs on many levels had not been met for a very long time. She yearned to experience the mutual understanding that comes from establishing a deeper, soulful connection. Instead, Vicki described feeling an ongoing sense of awkwardness with Ben. Many of the things that he said and did seemed foreign and uncomfortable to her—even after thirty-three years! Vicki rarely felt as though she and Ben were "on the same page" in their relationship.

For example, Vicki described the very different ways in which each of them related to sex. "Ben needs to get right down to business. The act of intercourse is the most important component. I need to experience lovemaking. Touching, caressing, kissing, and being intuitively connected with my partner is just as important as the act itself. Sometimes it's not just about achieving an orgasm." Even after several years of explaining to Ben how she felt, he didn't seem to get it. Ben's occasional attempts to understand and relate to Vicki ended in his impatience and self-expressed frustration.

Vicki originally came to me because she was still struggling with what to do. She and Ben had recently separated even though they maintained amicable and regular contact. Vicki continued to talk with Ben, expressing her hopes that he would make certain changes in order that they could finally have the kind of relationship that she had always wanted. Ben, on the other hand, resisted any attempts at change. He was adamant that he was quite happy with the way things were, including with who he was.

Ultimately, it was important for Vicki to make a decision in order to move forward in her life. Together, we discussed what it would mean to continue living her life with Ben as she had always done. We also discussed what life would be like if she were to move on from Ben.

It was almost as if there was this invisible line that existed for Vicki. On one side was where she had lived the majority of her life with Ben. On the other side of this imaginary line, Vicki saw her extreme happiness. Since separating from Ben, she had begun pursuing a Masters Degree in Education in order to embark on a new career teaching French. She had always been a voracious reader, and Vicki enjoyed introspective discussions on books that she was reading with colleagues and friends. She began planning a trip to Africa, a place she had longed to visit. She appeared to have an unquenchable energy and enthusiasm that leaped out at me whenever she spoke.

On the side of the line where she had spent much of her married life, Vicki admitted that it no longer felt comfortable. In fact, it felt painfully difficult to continue seeing and communicating with Ben when nothing was changing. Vicki admitted that she wasn't being true to herself by hoping Ben would change so she could have the kind of relationship she had always envisioned.

Through our work together, Vicki began to make the connection between all of the decisions that she made with her heart, which created the expansive feeling of being, as she put it, "bigger than I am." This was in direct contrast to the knee-jerk response of rationalizing her initial thoughts in order to make decisions based on what she thought she "should" do. Vicki noticed that by following her head as opposed to her heart, she began to feel closed, as though her heart had somehow shriveled up inside of her.

In a relationship that has completed its purpose, going forward may mean going it alone. Although they often last for long periods of time, love relationships are not necessarily destined to last "forever." Whereas society and religion tell us that marriage should last "till death do us part," the reality is that the relationships that you begin in your twenties or early thirties (when many people make the decision to marry) cannot always be expected to sustain and nurture your emotional, spiritual, and intellectual growth for the next forty years or more. Recognizing the immense benefit of each of your love relationships in teaching you valuable lessons, and embracing the notion that your first love may not endure your entire lifetime means that you can give yourself permission to end a relationship that feels completed.

慓

In love relationships, it is frequently common that one person may be willing to move outside of their comfort zone, to change and evolve, while the other partner may not be ready or even willing to look at self-change, for fear of the unknown or for what it might mean to do so. In the case where only one person in the relationship is willing to make some needed changes, it becomes very difficult for the relationship to evolve.

If it begins to feel as though you are fighting an uphill battle to achieve fundamental happiness, listen to your gut. You ultimately know when your love relationship has fatal flaws. It may be that your needs are consistently not being met, that there are critical differences and unresolved issues that make the relationship far too demanding of your time and resources, or that your relationship no longer contributes to the overall quality of your life.

It is at these pivotal moments that you must be honest with yourself even when it seems easier to continue on in the relationship. Seeing a professional therapist can help you recognize when it is time to create an exit strategy and how to move forward successfully once you are on your own. Knowing that it doesn't have to be about finding fault or blame with yourself or your partner, means that you can walk away with your eyes wide open and your head high.

Ending points are also important for teaching us that we can go on and we can thrive independently of our relationship. While it is ideal for a relationship to end on mutually agreeable terms, we are not always prepared for the imminent ending of our relationships. Of course, we also experience feelings of loss and confusion when we are not in agreement that a love relationship should end.

Relationships' endings provide turning points in your life. How you perceive these endings affects how you view yourself, what you look for in a partner, and how you will interact in your next relationship. Therefore, the end of a relationship can provide several important life lessons. Quite often, the inherent lesson in allowing a relationship to end is trusting that you will find another partner with whom to grow and evolve.

Making It Work

What about all of the couples who make it? They live together lovingly, not without their share of problems or issues but having the resolve to work at their relationship, navigating the rough spots, but also benefiting from having chosen a partner based on what they most wanted. These couples may or may not have attended individual or couple counseling at some point in their lives, but they certainly needed to practice good communication, respect, compassion, honesty, understanding, healthy self-esteem, and a satisfying sex life. Chances are they also practice conscious awareness in order to continue learning about themselves, and from their mistakes.

Couples who continue to be in love and flourishing after decades of being together are the ones that might be worth studying. After all, it is these particular love relationships that we can learn more from. While some people may argue that love relationships have a greater chance of survival with a formal contract of marriage, it is actually the personal commitment that both people in a healthy love relationship make to each other and their relationship that is a greater predictor of its overall success.

One of the tell tale signs of the strength of a love relationship is in what you do in the midst of a conflict. What happens each time the permanence of a relationship is threatened is critical to its future potential. On those occasions where a disagreement unleashes into a full blown, earth-shattering, fight, and yet both parties remain actively committed to their relationship (and to rebuilding and moving forward), you not only recover (with some time and further mending), but there is an incredible sense that the love relationship can withstand the difficult times without coming unglued. Equally significant is the knowledge that both members of a couple can continue on – hopefully having learned valuable lessons that don't need repeating.

Even as the truth can sometimes hurt, like the adage suggests, it also "sets you free." The one thing that will allow you and your partner to talk about the difficult issues in your everyday lives, as well as during times of conflict, is to always speak the truth. Of course, in the midst of heated discussions, when the method of delivery is less than ideal, the truth can be daringly painful to hear. And yet, if you can both come together and talk about what was said, sharing your thoughts and feelings about the real issues – with honesty – you can then have incredible, ground-breaking discussions. With compassion, forgiveness, and the solid commitment to reach a softer landing place, you and your partner will eventually reach a level of legitimate understanding that comes from saying exactly what is on your mind – no sugar coating, no skirting of issues, no holding your real feelings back – just truth.

Without being so overzealous as to think that you will always be perfectly happy with your partner, hopefully you have done enough homework at the outset so that over the course of time in relationship together, you will love your partner more. You can also reach a point where you no longer hope or pray that your love relationship will continue and thrive, you simply know that you will be together—and happy—forever.

Chapter Eight

A Soul Mate Relationship

A soul mate relationship brings two kindred spirits together with the exceptional purpose of cultivating healing and emotional and spiritual growth.

What was it exactly that first attracted you to your current love relationship? What was the specific appeal that compelled you to want to know this person more than any other?

How are we sometimes able to establish an instantly recognizable, and often compelling, connection with a particular individual? How is it that some relationships are easy and effortless while others can require an inordinate amount of work and energy often without similar results?

"Soul Mates"

Transcending religions, philosophies, cultures, and civilizations is the belief that the universe is governed by a set of indestructible, inescapable laws, referred to as the Laws of the Universe. Supported by scientific evidence, the Laws of the Universe define our physical existence. The first of these, the Law of Conservation of Energy, defined in quantum physics, describes energy as existing in all matter. It may flow into or out of one form or another, but energy can neither be created nor destroyed.

Adopted from the current literature on New Age mysticism, the term "soul mates" refers to elements of spiritual and religious traditions, integrated with ideas from modern science. Modern-day mystics explain soul mates as two individuals who have unconscious or soul memories of previous experiences being in relationship.

Since energy is neither created nor destroyed, the energy or life force within each of us goes somewhere when our physical bodies die. Whether your life force returns to an originating source—a universal life force—or, as proposed by ancient theories of reincarnation, it is reborn into a new body, it is conceivable that the life force within you has previously been a part of a different living being—obviously from a different time and place.

Child music prodigies or children gifted in disciplines of math or science when they have received little or no formal training serve to support the central tenet of reincarnation that some part of the being remains constantly present throughout successive lives.

You may have known your soul mate in a past lifetime as a sibling, parent, friend, or lover. Regardless of the previous relationship, what remains important is that you are reacquainted with this person (and their life force). You do not likely recognize the physical attributes of this person, nor the particular relationship dynamics, because they would be very different from the previous time. What you feel oddly reacquainted with is the life force that you once knew. This would explain how soul mates feel instinctively drawn to one another. Soul mates experience a definitively familiar, yet intangible connection that compels them to want to know each other further in this lifetime.

A soul mate relationship brings two kindred spirits together with the exceptional purpose of cultivating healing and emotional and spiritual growth. Unlike any other relationship, a soul mate relationship offers a profound connection with a partner who embraces all of who you are—as you are.

Soul mate love relationships embody spiritual growth. It is through your intuitive pursuit of greater wisdom and life purpose that you look for a partner with similar philosophical views and beliefs. A soul mate relationship is an evolved relationship and therefore is possible only when you live your life with authenticity and integrity of spirit. Being committed to your self-evolution means that you seek out a soul mate partnership with someone who can support and honor your spiritual journey. Quite possibly your partner may also be inspired to pursue their own truth. (It is not uncommon for one partner in a couple to begin their own personal journey on a timeline similar to the other.)

In addition to the possibility of being in love with your soul mate, soul mate relationships can exist among best friends, siblings, and between parent and child. They are not limited to one person at any one time. Soul mate relationships are typically long lasting, spanning several decades if not your entire lifetime. The prevailing notion is that soul mates play a profound and explicitly meaningful role in each other's lives. They are intentionally re-united in this lifetime in order to help each other "heal" and to become whole. While you may have the benefit of experiencing several soul mate relationships in your lifetime, it is through being in love with your soul mate that you experience the greatest potential for self-fulfillment and self-actualization.

Characteristics of a Soul Mate Love Relationship

Your soul mate love relationship is uniquely characterized by the following qualities:

1) An immediate feeling of ease and comfort in the presence of your soul mate. You easily share personal information and opinions, and feel free to be exactly who you are.

With a soul mate, you feel comfortable and at ease from the very first contact. Since it is "safe" to let your guard down, you are able to share honestly about yourself, including your expectations for a relationship, your dreams and ambitions. Once in relationship, soul mates identify a consistent theme of familiarity. This relaxed feeling is described as being like "having known each other before."

2) A profound and meaningful connection that effortlessly transcends ordinary communication.

In a soul mate love relationship, communicating, and relating is effortless: it occurs naturally, as if by some infinite grace. Your philosophical conversations cover a broad range of topics. They expand past everyday communication to enlighten and provoke creative thought and intellectual discussion. In sharing their innate wisdom and ideas, soul mates also provide each other with divine guidance. Your soul mate has the uncanny ability to say just the right thing—offering advice or insight—in moments when you need it the most.

3) The experience of unconditional love.

A soul mate love relationship fosters love without conditions or limits. Soul mates are able to give and receive unconditional love, continually and unequivocally. They express and experience love and devotion in many forms.

Developing such a close affinity offers the soul mate couple an inescapable mechanism for progressing forward in their own self-directed growth. It is through being in relationship with a soul mate, that you feel embraced in an exceptional type of love, a love that reaffirms your place in the world and in who you are. Your soul mate love relationship offers a deeper connection to your self, allowing you to realize your true potential.

That soul mates can love one another so fully and completely, without sacrificing their self in the process, is one of the richest and most fulfilling experiences of life.

4) An inherent knowing that your soul mate completes you.

Your soul mate inspires you to become a better human being. You are challenged to grow beyond what you have previously thought possible—to be more.

Being in relationship together, you and your soul mate challenge each other to examine the aspects of your lives that you are less than happy with. As part of your already growing consciousness, you recognize the limits that maintaining old behaviors impose on you and you seek out ways of changing and improving. Your soul mate environment supports your desire for change and improvement. Your soul mate's ability to empower, inspire, support, and encourage you is limitless.

Soul mates are attracted to specific traits in one another that they have not entirely developed in their self. For example, not only do you find it appealing that your soul mate is outgoing and sociable, but it is through being in relationship, that you feel inspired to develop these qualities in yourself. In doing so, you realize the benefit of being more comfortable (and even confident) in a variety of different social settings, something that you previously did not feel skilled at.

Your soul mate has the ability to offer you a true reflection of how you actually are. It is through compassionately pointing out your flaws (and in many cases this information is not new to you but rather validates what you already suspect) that you are motivated to improve, grow, and become the person that you ideally desire to be.

As you feel safe to reveal all of your self with your soul mate, you can begin to heal. Knowing that you are accepted and loved regardless of your imperfections compels you to see yourself honestly and (to the best of your desires and capabilities) elicit desired changes in your search for becoming more.

5) A soul mate love relationship is a highly evolved relationship that presupposes full consciousness

A soul mate love relationship can exist only as the two individuals live with full consciousness. It is in practicing self-awareness that soul mates have the ability to see themselves and each other with clarity and truth.

Soul mates find each other in part because they choose to live with integrity. Their quest for living an authentic and fulfilling life enables them to search wholeheartedly for a life partner that will be best suited to them.

Soul Mates in Love —
A Spiritually Conscious Relationship

A spiritually conscious relationship requires that you actively seek inner wisdom, knowledge, and the greater meaning of your life. In their search for greater meaning and purpose, soul mates embrace a divine connection to the universal spirit. Soul mates listen and trust their intuitive wisdom to provide guidance and direction for their lives.

Soul mates in love have the propensity to develop the highest potential of authenticity of any relationship. Because of their history together from previous lifetimes, soul mates feel secure and safe to continue their spiritual growth—completely supported by their mutual love.

As soul mates live consciously, they recognize the importance of realizing and living their purpose. They evolve in their experience of "self" as individuals while simultaneously are challenged to grow.

Cultivating a Spiritually Conscious Love Relationship

Cultivate a spiritually conscious love relationship with your soul mate by embracing the following:

• Practice authenticity (be fully honest and "real") at all times, and encourage your mate to do so as well. Often one partner is more reserved about sharing their true thoughts and opinions, and, at times, may need encouraging to do so.

• Ensure that you spend time alone each day with your thoughts to connect within. (Close your eyes for three to five minutes and breathe.) Quiet is paramount in order to hear your inner voice. Practice listening to your inner voice, and experience the wisdom of knowing what is right and best for you.

- Encourage your soul mate to trust their intuitiveness as you trust yours. Share your intuitive thoughts and feelings with each other as a means of strengthening your connection.

- Provide mutual support and encouragement of each other's spiritual growth (e.g. spirituality practice, self-directed study, and so on). Seek to understand one another's spiritual beliefs and philosophical views.

- Use your immense capacity for forgiveness by letting go of hurts and grudges. This enables you to be able to love fully and completely. Use empathy and compassion to truly understand each other. Seek ultimately to forgive the person first and then their actions.

 G3

A love relationship with your soul mate is made possible by the considerable work you have done in evolving as an individual. You evolve as you seek opportunities to learn and grow, and as you remain committed to the process of developing a high level of consciousness.

To be conscious is to make choices consistent with your truth. You live authentically as you develop a greater connection with your inner self. Soul mates remain committed to their own individual growth by actively working on their relationship with "self"and their connection to their inner spirit. Because they maintain a strong sense of self, soul mates can support and love each other without giving up a part of who they are.

Soul mate love relationships allow for the evolution of your spirit. In being in a love relationship with your soul mate, you have the propensity to evolve in part because you have the love and support to pursue your individual purpose. You are comforted by the knowledge that your spiritual connection transcends the physical aspects of your soul mate relationship. You have the support and encouragement to become and achieve all that you desire.

Examine your existing relationships. Which have the hidden potential for being soul mate relationships? Often we have the experience of a soul mate relationship with a family member or a friend long before we find our soul mate love relationship. Recognizing the unique qualities and characteristics present in an existing soul mate relationship is important as you seek a soul mate life partner.

CB

I didn't believe in the possibility of soul mates until Ryan. It was only after being in relationship together for a considerable length of time, and after doing significant reading and research on the topic—exploring elements of spirituality and ideas of reincarnation as a widespread doctrine—that I thought more about the possibility.

It's likely that most people don't start out in a love relationship believing that they have met a soul mate. It's more realistic to expect that you need to spend significant time with a person before you can accurately begin to consider the prospect.

While there are a myriad of personal experiences that reinforce for people their soul mate connection, none are "incorrect." Most commonly, it is an unyielding feeling that simply allows you to know without any doubt, and usually coupled with an overwhelming feeling of calmness that stays with you, even during times of conflict, gently reminding you all of the more important reasons for being together in relationship. Maybe each of us needs a sign to know for sure that we have made the right decision in choosing a mate or when we have met our soul mate. Quite possibly, we do receive those signs and all that we need to do is pay attention.

A soul mate love relationship is indeed the greatest gift.

Chapter Nine

Lessons for Healing and Growth

Love allows you to heal. To operate from a place of love suggests that you have learned much about what it is that serves to nurture your self and others.

Learning is infinite and continuous. To recognize and learn the life lessons that are an inherent part of being in a love relationship creates incredible possibilities for who you become. If you consider all of your life experiences as opportunities for learning and personal growth, you no longer need to resist situations that present themselves, or feel defeated by events that you cannot control.

A healthy, nurturing love relationship provides you with a safe and supportive environment in which to explore your fears, inadequacies, and self doubts. In an environment of trust and acceptance, you know it is safe to be authentic. You can allow your partner to see all of you and trust that you will still be loved. This does not excuse you from behaving badly, but rather it gives you the freedom to show sides of yourself that you normally would hide from the rest of the world.

Your ability to heal while in a love relationship occurs most deeply when you have unconditional love, truth, honesty, and acceptance. It is the element of unconditional love (love that is given freely and without requirements) that nurtures you, allowing you to shed your insecurities. It is not until you are able to be "real," completely honest and truthful, with yourself and your partner, and eventually others that your self-directed journey of growth truly begins.

Healing your spirit requires you to relinquish control of the facade that you have created for the outside world. If you are fortunate enough to have a family of origin that values honesty, truth, and integrity, then it is likely that you have already (whether consciously or unconsciously) looked for those values in your love relationship. If these values were present in your initial family, then it is more likely that you have learned (at least to some degree) how to be honest with yourself about who you are.

Unfortunately, if you were raised in an environment of mistrust, abuse, or the absence of unconditional love, it is crucial that you find healthy examples of love, acceptance and truth to model yourself on. Support to assist your healing may come through books, seeking professional help, or through the encouragement and love of the healthy relationships that you surround yourself with. Together, the elements of unconditional love, truth, honesty, and acceptance allow you to accomplish your personal journey of self-actualization.

As you remain true to who you are and what you believe in, the universe supports you in your quest for a higher consciousness. You begin to find others who also practice authenticity, and with whom you feel a profound connection. These positive, supportive, relationships validate your need to be fully authentic. This validation furthers your personal healing and growth.

Life Lessons from Your Love Relationship

In your initial love relationships, as an adolescent, you choose someone who (on an unconscious level) has qualities similar to that of either or both parents in your family of origin. Quite frequently, what you find most appealing in this person is also largely intangible. In your initial love relationships, you experience a familiarity that is coupled with a physical attraction.

If asked what it was exactly that attracted you to this particular person, you would most likely describe characteristics and physical attributes that you find appealing. (e.g. "They have a beautiful smile" or "I love how strong and muscular they are.") And yet, when you look beyond the physical to acknowledge what it is that you most love about this particular person, the answer might sound something more like: "I know my boyfriend really cares about me because of the way he looks at me and how he treats me," or "She really seems to understand me. She listens when I rant about my family, and it feels good to know that I can talk to my girlfriend about anything." These are the elusive behaviors and traits that more accurately appeal to your sense of familiarity—to what you have known and experienced growing up.

Your first experiences of being in love offer support and validation of your developing self-worth. They are also important in teaching you resilience since breakups and heartache are integral components of these initial love relationships.

As your emotional and psychological self develops, and as you experience growth in your self-confidence, you begin to look for different qualities in a prospective partner. As you evolve, your sense of self is an important determinant in what you now look for in a love relationship.

If, in your family of origin, you did not receive the emotional and psychological nurturing that fosters self-love and autonomy, you will continue to seek emotional and psychological nurturing and support in each of your love relationships. Lacking the fundamental ability to establish your place in the world and to develop a healthy sense of self makes it extremely difficult to give of yourself in relationship.

In this case, your relationships (particularly your love relationships) become a place of refuge from the outside world. Your love relationship (and particularly your mate) continues to be the primary source of your emotional and psychological well-being. Those who grew up without a loving childhood environment (and the feeling of connectedness that is experienced in receiving unconditional love) continue to search for this type of love in the relationships that they form. Without emotional and psychological nurturing to foster a sense of security and autonomy, you are less likely to explore your world and to perceive life events positively, thereby not developing confidence and self-worth.

Unfortunately, the void of these experiences in childhood can never be filled. As an adult, it is up to you to provide yourself with the emotional support and resilience that you perhaps did not receive in childhood, even though you would not have formally learned how to go within to provide this for yourself. Hence, you rely on external sources for your feelings of adequacy and self-worth.

CS

Since all of us carry emotional wounds from our past, we look to our love relationships in an unconscious attempt to heal. As part of the inherent bliss that embodies the experience of love, each successive love relationship has the potential to offer us further healing, in part because of the love we receive and in part from our ability in being loved, to heal ourselves.

1) You are able to heal issues from your past in your family of origin.

Because most of us are not aware of the intricate wounds that we carry from childhood, we cannot recognize when our love relationships offer us an opportunity to heal from these wounds, and instead we become mired in repeating the entire drama all over again.

For example, my client Ann began therapy because she wanted a place to explore issues that were affecting her self-confidence in relationships with men. At twenty-seven, Ann was a junior at a progressive law firm. Remarkably intelligent, she had easily impressed others and earned a reputation as a quick study. Ann would demonstrate her devotion to her work by frequently taking on additional files and always going above and beyond what was expected in order to please the firm's partners.

As Ann began to describe the status of her love life, however, it became clear that she operated with a core belief of being "not good enough." Ann confessed that she had never had a serious love relationship and that "no man was ever 'in love' with her." While

Ann enjoyed her career, having numerous friends and a great apartment in the city, she admitted that she wanted more than just casual relationships with the men she met.

The one man that Ann was seeing at the moment was not committed to her. She explained that they would see each other casually for sex—mostly at his request. While Ann's feelings for this man were growing, it was clear that he did not want to pursue a love relationship. Ann admitted that she continued with their casual encounters in the hope that he would one day "want something more permanent." In the meantime, she felt dejected since the men that Ann found herself most attracted to didn't reciprocate her feelings.

We learn about love relationships from our parents (as well as our observations of our parents' relationship with each other). This template becomes the "norm" for how we behave and what we expect in our relationships with others. The underlying messages that you received from your family of origin, determine your existing learned beliefs.

Ann noted that her father had suffered from bouts of clinical depression for most of her life. Her father's chronic history of moodiness coupled with critical self-doubt meant that Ann "learned" how to "make her father feel better" by offering to do things to cheer him up. Ann recognized that she had purposely set out to be a "good girl," doing what she thought would make her father happy in order to receive his praise. Seeing a smile on his face and knowing that she had contributed to her father's momentary happiness made Ann feel special. It became evident that Ann's learned way of relating with her father was a predominant factor in how she perceived her role in love relationships.

With men, Ann realized that she would go out of her way to make herself available and to please them. She would often have casual sex (even hours after meeting someone for the first time) because as things progressed through the course of the evening she believed that saying "no" would cause them to become angry with her. In giving so much of herself so freely, Ann never gained their respect. In convincing herself that men would like her if she did what she believed they wanted, Ann rarely did what was right for her. Ann operated in a way that she had learned would please others first, only to feel exploited and saddened when her efforts did not work. Ann's core belief—that she wasn't good enough to have someone interested in her—continued to be reinforced.

Once Ann recognized that her current behavior with men was related, and in fact, largely based on what she inherently learned as a child, she was able to change that behavior. Ann and I worked on challenging her core belief and creating a healthy alternative, based on what was accurate. Together, we also developed strategies for building her self-worth, and Ann initiated ideas that would help her to feel better about her physical attractiveness, something that she highlighted as specifically important to her.

As Ann worked on the aspects of her self that needing attention, she was finally able to let go of feeling "not good enough." As her self-confidence and self-worth grew stronger, Ann was able to enjoy the experience of meeting and dating men, but with careful attention to whether or not they were someone that would be suited for her. Ann no longer felt a need to please others in order to be liked. She acknowledged the importance of having someone like her for who she was.

2) Your most intimate relationships provide you with the mechanism to learn valuable life lessons.

Your most significant relationships, regardless of whether they are romantic, familial, or between best friends, will continue to present you with important life lessons until you finally master them. By paying careful attention, especially to ongoing challenges and unresolved conflict, you begin to identify the life lessons that you need to learn. Mastering these lessons means that you can apply and integrate what you have learned in any number of given situations over the rest of your life. These life lessons are integral to your ability to grow and evolve as a human being.

To think that you "keep meeting the same type of women," or that "every man you have ever loved has hurt you like this!" is really the universe providing you with ample opportunities to learn valuable lessons about ways of being. When you don't pay attention to the lessons the universe places in front of you, you invariably find yourself repeating familiar patterns and experiencing similar difficult situations.

Ending a love relationship as a way of avoiding the uncomfortable challenges you face, only assures that these same lessons will show up again in future relationships. That is what happened to my client Jason.

Jason, 39, had recently moved in with his girlfriend of fifteen months. He spoke about Nicole as the first woman to come along in several years that he was truly "in love" with. Jason admitted that he'd spent most of his thirties focusing on his career and dating either casually or not much at all and he acknowledged that each of his three previous relationships had lasted only a few of months at best. Jason recognized that his typical pattern was to end a relationship rather than attempt to resolve the conflict when it arouse.

Jason began therapy in the hopes of working on aspects of himself, in order to move past the issues that had surfaced with Nicole. He was eager to understand the reasons for his intense feelings of sadness and anger every time he and Nicole had any kind of disagreement. Nicole, who Jason described as having a strong personality, was not shy about expressing her thoughts and feelings, even though at times, it meant expressing distinctly different views from Jason. If Jason felt angry or hurt, he would typically become withdrawn and avoid any further conversation. This would frustrate Nicole, making it almost impossible for the two of them to resolve issues.

Your love relationships provide you with opportunities to explore those aspects of your self that remain problematic, and to challenge you to grow beyond what you have always done. Being in a committed love relationship makes it far more difficult to dismiss your true feelings and thoughts for fear of creating conflict: you may be able to leave your environment temporarily (slamming the door as you exit), but ultimately the desire to continue in your relationship challenges you to find a more effective way of dealing with problems and issues.

Avoiding or denying your true emotions creates inner conflict. You are able to co-exist in your love relationship for only so long before the mounting inner angst reaches an impasse. Issues that have been buried because they can't be resolved resurface repeatedly as similar incidents occur, and as one or both partners continue to build underlying resentment and anger.

Applying the Cognitive Therapy tool: THOUGHTS ➡ FEELINGS ➡ BEHAVIORS at times when he felt sad reminded Jason that his thoughts determined his feelings.

Case Example:

Jason's thoughts in moments of conflict with Nicole:

"I can't believe she made such a mess in the kitchen!"
"How come she has to use every single pot we have?"
"I can't handle her cooking for me if it means creating such a disaster."
"I'm going to have to clean this mess up!"
"I can't live like this."
"This is insane. ... What am I doing in this relationship?"

Understanding that he was responsible for creating his feelings, Jason began to observe his thoughts especially at times when he and Nicole had minor disagreements. Jason began to challenge his initial thoughts particularly as he realized that he had made various assumptions, creating his own story of what he thought Nicole was saying or inferred. Creating a story meant that Jason would interpret something Nicole said in a particular way based on his own view of the world, his beliefs, current mood state, and previous life experiences. Rather than check it out to make sure that his "story" was valid, Jason would assume that his interpretation was entirely accurate.

Challenging Jason's initial thoughts by creating a more accurate version of the truth:

"I can't believe she made such a mess in the kitchen!" ➡
"I know she's trying her best. I know she didn't make a mess on purpose."
"How come she has to use every single pot we have?" ➡
"She really hasn't used every pot" (Jason's exaggeration of the situation).
"I can't handle her cooking for me if it means creating such a disaster." ➡ **"Maybe we can have a conversation about this.**

I really enjoy her cooking, so maybe we can figure out a way for her to clean up a bit as she goes along."

"I'm going to have to clean this mess up!" ➡

"I actually don't mind cleaning up if she does the cooking. I like a clean and organized kitchen."

"I can't live like this." ➡

"I really love living with her, so I'm going to work on figuring out a way to be okay with the way she cooks."

"This is insane. ... What am I doing in this relationship?" ➡

"I love Nicole and our relationship. I don't want to lose her."

Using the tool THOUGHTS ➡ FEELINGS ➡ BEHAVIORS, allowed Jason to overcome the unpleasant thoughts and feelings that would previously have provoked him to simply walk away from his love relationship.

In his commitment to remaining in the relationship and working through the challenges of communicating at times when he felt angry or sad, Jason was learning valuable information about himself.

Being willing to explore, and ultimately understand, his thoughts during minor disagreements with Nicole, Jason began to recognize the connection between his thoughts and interpretation of a particular issue, and his feelings of anger or sadness. As Jason became more skilled at observing and challenging his thoughts and to ask questions—clarifying what Nicole actually said rather than assume the worst—he noticed that his feelings were far more manageable. Jason could now appropriately resolve many of his irrational thoughts, rather than allow them to affect how he felt and behaved.

You have the potential to make important discoveries in moments when you experience reoccurring disagreements or conflicts by taking a close look at the patterns that emerge. If you continue to face similar types of conflict, it is largely because you have not yet learned how to think about, and behave differently in those situations. You learn from any ongoing issues or disagreements in your relationships, by exploring your behaviors and actions as well as the particular way in which you think.

Conflicts or disagreements are the obvious starting place to look for life lessons. Conflicts challenge your inner resources. When you are faced with a disagreement or conflict in a love relationship, you are challenged to navigate through it. Some of us can do this successfully while most others feel ill equipped to handle the uncomfortable feelings that go along with conflict. Starting with your thoughts, examine your style of relating when you experience conflict, as a first step in considering what life lesson may be awaiting you.

❧

Ultimately, a conflict within your love relationship suggests that you need to think differently about a particular issue. Challenge your pre-conceived ideas about what you think is true or right and, instead, seek to truly understand.

When you approach challenges from a place of "What do I need to be doing differently here?" or "What is the lesson here for me?" it means that you have stepped out of your usual pattern of being. By looking at the situation from a position of learning, you can feel empowered to make changes to the way in which you think, feel, and react.

By challenging yourself to practice new behaviors, you will notice changes in the way in which you and your partner relate to one another. Seeing even the smallest change in the outcome of a particular exchange between you and your partner offers hope that you have the ability to create positive circumstances by choosing how you are.

3) Your potential for positive growth and healing are invariably based on your willingness to be consciously aware.

In choosing to remain consciously aware in all aspects of your life, you become purposeful in your actions and choices. You see the importance of creating positive experiences for yourself and in your varied relationships with others.

When you ignore your innate knowledge of what is right and best based on your individual needs, you no longer operate from a place of consciousness. As you go through life, disengaged from your spirit, you relinquish your sense of self. Remaining unconscious allows you to simply co-exist in your relationship indefinitely, rather than be motivated and inspired by your desire for greater happiness. After a period of time, you move further away from what your self needs in order to be happy. You lose touch with your spirit and feel further disconnected from within. Over time, you no longer remember how to cultivate happiness based on what you know to be right for you. You replace self with others and you focus on the successes and accomplishments of those around you all the while further disconnecting from your core self.

"Love" Lessons

Examine the life lessons inherent in your previous or current love relationship. Answer the following questions as honestly as possible, recording your answers in detail. (You can always build on your answers as you recall additional information and ideas.)

1.) What are some of the most significant lessons I have learned about myself through being in relationship with this person?

_____

_____

_____

2.) How have I changed as a result of being in this relationship? How have these changes supported my becoming a more evolved and complete human being?

_____

_____

_____

3.) What common issues continue to surface again and again without resolution in my relationship?

_____

_____

_____

4.) What are the typical ways in which I react to these conflicts?

_____

_____

_____

5.) How do I need to respond in order to create a positive outcome in this situation?

_____

_____

_____

6.) What would happen if I were to respond in this more positive way most of the time?

_____

_____

_____

In reviewing your responses to the above questions, what does this information tell you?

_____

_____

_____

Finally....

7.) What behaviors do you still need to change in order to further improve your love relationship?

_____

_____

_____

8.) What lessons do you still need to learn in order to heal?

_____

_____

_____

9.) Is this a love relationship that is truly right and best for you? Why? / Why not?

_____

_____

_____

Each of your love relationships is purposeful in teaching you about your self. In being open to learning from your experiences, you grow, evolve, and heal. It then becomes easier to choose your relationships because you choose differently, based on who you have become. Knowing that all of your love relationships are not necessarily meant to be forever is important if you are committed to finding the best suitable partner.

⋐

Trust that you will be presented with a particular life lesson at a time when you have the capacity to learn it and not before. In fact, you may be in the same relationship for some time, before a specific life lesson is presented to you. Unfortunately, you may also find yourself struggling to master a particular life lesson for months or even years, since some lessons are more difficult to learn than others. Like any new skill, learning a life lesson requires on-going practice and effort.

Ultimately, a learned life lesson must be felt in the heart. You must experience a deep sense of knowing, of inner confidence within yourself that if presented with a similar situation again in the future, then you will not resort back to old patterns of behaving. I like to think of it as being "tested" in the mastery of what you have learned. Mastering a life lesson is truly moving forward; it is about not repeating the same mistakes over again.

Healing Your Past

You carry with you all of your old hurts and sorrows from previous experiences, events, and past relationships, as well as your current need to be loved and cared for. How you identify and interpret all of your earlier wounds affects how your need to be loved by another overtakes your ability to provide that love for yourself.

Your commitment to healing the hurts of your past makes all the difference between finding a love relationship in which those earlier wounds continue to affect you, and one in which you can accept and embrace all of the new experiences and events that are offered.

Both people in a love relationship will be challenged to work on issues from their past. How successful you are depends to a large degree on your sense of self (your inner confidence and self-worth) as well as the strength of your relationship, including the support and love of your partner.

You will be most successful at healing from your past when you can identify and acknowledge the hurts and wounds that are there and then have the desire to let them go. Without conscious awareness, your past often predicts your present. Without being aware of what you need to heal from your past, you continue living as you have always done, repeating the same patterns of behaving, reacting in the same way to situations, and feeling all of the same emotions as a result. Inevitably, nothing changes. In fact, you continue to gather more hurts and wounds throughout your life until you start to feel the physical effects of your never-addressed emotional pain.

To release some of the emotional pain of your past, create a list of the emotional wounds that you continue to hold onto. Begin with your initial relationships in your family of origin. For example, maybe you felt as though you were treated differently in some way to your siblings. (For some people, this may actually be true.)

However, if when growing up, you began to develop the belief that you were disciplined more severely for your mistakes than your younger siblings, or if you believe you were at times reared by a different set of rules than your other siblings, you instinctively look for examples in your past that support this belief. Because you continue to look for evidence that fits your view of your past, your perception of all future situations and events becomes somewhat biased. You also tend to overlook and diminish those past incidents in which you were treated fairly or given preferential treatment simply because they don't fit your pre-established belief system.

As you carry a core belief into your adult life, you continue to unconsciously look for events and circumstances that further strengthen it. Your belief that others always find fault with you cannot help but affect all of your current relationships including those in which you are in love.

Similarly, maybe you believe that your parents loved you, but with conditions. (Whether this is actually true or not is less important than the fact that you believe it to be true.) Your parents may have unknowingly created an "if … then" rule by making expressions of love and affection conditional on doing things that they valued. Your core belief may be that positive praise and attention was given only when you met certain criteria or expectations of your parents. For example, praise and attention may have been given for looking a certain way, getting good grades, being "good" in the presence of adults, and so on.

Acknowledge all of these well-ingrained beliefs (these wounds), by listing them below. Also acknowledge how they affected your life. For example, how do you behave in your present love relationship if you believe that love is conditional? How do you react in your present relationships if you believe that you have to be a certain way in order to be deemed "good enough"?

Case Example:

The Life Situations that I Believe to be True:

1. I was unfairly disciplined by my parents.
   i.e. My parents were harder on me than on my siblings. I received punishment more frequently (for minor incidents) while my siblings' bad behavior was frequently overlooked.

2. Love was given with conditions.
   i.e. If I did what my parents wanted, I would receive positive support and acceptance. I learned how to receive praise and positive rewards by being good.

The Impact of my Life Situations on Present-Day Relationships:

1. I often assume that my partner is criticizing me when he claims he is only making a suggestion or sharing his perspective about something. I get defensive easily when my partner says something I have done is wrong, and I argue my position emphatically. Because of this, our discussions often lead to conflict.

2. I always ask my partner what I should do before making an important decision. I usually don't do what I really want for fear of making a "wrong" decision, and causing her to be upset with me.

Acknowledge that the wounds that continue to affect you come directly from your perceptions and knowledge of earlier life experiences. Identifying your core beliefs as the source of these wounds is a first step towards healing. Healing your wounds requires you to actively work on changing your core beliefs and to practice forgiveness (of yourself and others) as you begin to see your situation from different perspectives.

Healing Your Present

In an extraordinary way, your ability to heal comes most predominantly from your ability to operate with love each day. There is opportunity to love and nurture your inner self most as you listen inwardly to your spirit. Know that your inner voice directs you out of the highest good to honor your best self.

On the many occasions that you will make mistakes and will falter, your best guarantee in creating healthy relationships in all areas of your life is to consistently work on becoming a better person. Your dedication to healing those parts of you that have been wounded, and to operating with greater compassion and understanding of others, requires ongoing practice and effort. To master these elements is to re-establish your ties to your self and your inner spirit. From within, anything is possible.

Recommended Reading

Beck, Aaron T. *Love Is Never Enough: How Couples Can Overcome Misunderstandings, Resolve Conflicts, and Solve Relationship Problems through Cognitive Therapy.* Harper Collins Canada Ltd, 1989.

Branden, Nathaniel. *The Psychology of Romantic Love.* Bantam Books, 1985.

Greenberger, Dennis. and Christine Padesky. *Mind Over Mood: A Cognitive Therapy Treatment Manual for Clients.* The Guilford Press, 1995.

Hendrix, Harville. *Getting the Love You Want: A Guide for Couples.* Atna, 2003.

Hendrix, Harville. *Keeping the Love You Find.* Atna, 1993.

Joudry, Patricia and Maurie Pressman. *Twin Souls: Finding Your True Spiritual Partner.* Hazelden, 2000.

Lama Surya Das. *Awakening to the Sacred: Creating a Personal Spiritual Life.* Broadway Books, 1999.

Miguel Ruiz, Don. *The Mastery of Love: A Practical Guide to the Art of Relationship.* Amber-Allen Publishing, 1999.

Moore, Thomas. *Soul Mates: Honoring the Mysteries of Love and Relationship.* Wheeler Publishing. 1994.

Scarf, Maggie. *Intimate Partners: Patterns in Love and Marriage.* Ballantine Books, 1987.

Zukav, Gary. *Soul Stories.* Free Press, 2000.

Index

About the Author

Dorothy Ratusny is a psychotherapist in private practice in Toronto, Canada. She works with both individual and couple clients, utilizing a Cognitive Therapy model. In addition to her private practice, Dorothy facilitates personalized corporate training sessions and speaks on a range of topics to professional groups and organizations.

Dorothy was featured on the Life Network as host of the 13-week television documentary series, *Love Is Not Enough*. The series followed the unfolding drama of four couples as they worked to overcome unresolved issues and improve their relationships. More recently, she has been co-host of *Womyn's Word* on CHRY 105.5 FM Radio in Toronto.

Dorothy writes for a number of publications and newspapers, and has been a guest on CTV's Talk TV: *The Chat Room*, CFRB 1010AM (Toronto), AM640 (Toronto), CJAD 800 AM (Montreal), The Life Network's Canadian Living Television, Rogers' *Daytime*, The Discovery Health Network's *Health on the Line*, City TV's *Breakfast Television*, *Cable Pulse 24*, TVO's *Studio Two*, TLN's *Viva Domenica*, and SLICE's *Three Takes*.